079337

 day

D1356314

Dark Tourism

Dark Tourism

John Lennon
and Malcolm Foley

CONTINUUM
London and New York

Continuum
The Tower Building, 11 York Road, London SE1 7NX
370 Lexington Avenue, New York, NY 10017-6503

First published 2000

British Library Cataloguing-in-Publication Data
A catalogue record for this book is available from the British Library.

ISBN   0 8264 5063 6 (hardback)
       0 8264 5064 4 (paperback)

Designed and typeset by Ben Cracknell Studios

Printed and bound in Great Britain by TJ International, Padstow, Cornwall

Contents

Illustrations   vi

Chapter One   Intimations of Dark Tourism   1

Chapter Two   Instances of Dark Tourism   13

Chapter Three   The Third Reich and the Final Solution   27

Chapter Four   The Death Camps of Poland   46

Chapter Five   Covering History: The Interpretation of
                 the Channel Islands Occupation, 1939–45   66

Chapter Six   The Death Site of a President   77

Chapter Seven   War Sites of the First and Second World Wars   99

Chapter Eight   North Cyprus: Disappointing Performance
                 with 'Dark' Edges   129

Chapter Nine   Dislocation: The US Holocaust
                 Memorial Museum   145

Chapter Ten   The Future of Dark Tourism: From the
                 Final Solution to the End of History   162

                 Bibliography   170

                 Index   180

Illustrations

1	Vietnam Vets Memorial, Washington	15
2	Korean Vets Memorial, Washington	15
3	Plötzensee Memorial, Berlin	36
4	House of the Wannsee Conference, Berlin	38
5	Sachsenhausen KZ, Berlin	41
6	Dissecting table, Sachsenhausen KZ, Berlin	43
7	Olympia Stadium, Berlin	45
8	Auschwitz KZ, Oswieczim, Poland	48
9	Gates of Auschwitz II, Birkenau KZ, Oswieczim, Poland	51
10	Sign from Lidice, Czech Republic	54
11	Map of Auschwitz KZ, Oswieczim, Poland	56
12	Exhibit of Zyklon B gas canisters, Auschwitz KZ, Oswieczim, Poland	57
13	Site of crematoria, Auschwitz KZ, Oswieczim, Poland	59
14	Hair/shoes exhibit from Auschwitz KZ, Oswieczim, Poland	61
15	Gate and entrance, Borkum KZ, Alderney	70
16	German Underground Hospital, Jersey	71
17	Liberation Memorial, St Helier, Jersey	72
18	JFK Library, Boston, Massachusetts	81
19	The Sixth Floor (entrance), Dallas, Texas	82
20	The Eternal Flame, Arlington, Virginia	88
21	USS *Arizona* Memorial, Pearl Harbor, Honolulu, Hawaii	104
22	USS *Arizona* Memorial Museum, Pearl Harbor, Honolulu, Hawaii	107

23 Museum at Checkpoint Charlie, Berlin 114

24 Memorial to civil rights protestors at Birmingham, Alabama 115

25 Scene from Imperial War Museum, Duxford 117

26 Section of the Berlin Wall outside the Imperial War
Museum, London 121

27 British Memorial to the Battle of the Somme, Thiépval,
France 123

28 Sign on Tourist Trail, Normandy, France 126

29 First house liberated by Allied troops, Normandy, France 127

30 Border point, Turkish Republic of Northern Cyprus 138

31 Denktash image, City Square, Lefkosa, Turkish Republic of
Northern Cyprus 139

32 Forbidden Zone (Demilitarized Zone), Turkish Republic of
Northern Cyprus 142

33 Museum of Barbarism, Turkish Republic of Northern
Cyprus 143

34 US Holocaust Memorial Museum, Washington, DC 145

35 Museum of Tolerance at the Simon Wiesenthal Center,
Los Angeles 150

36 Vehicle used for Graveline Tours at Mann's Chinese Theater,
Los Angeles 165

Diagram 1 Matrix showing treatment of location in terms of
production and consumption 89

CHAPTER ONE

Intimations of Dark Tourism

The town of Bukittingi in West Sumatra was a resort mainly for Dutch colonial inhabitants of Indonesia prior to the establishment of a republic. It is located in beautiful countryside, with spectacular mountain ranges in the middle distance and breathtaking valleys and lakes in close proximity. The town itself is constructed on a hilltop which commands views across the hills and valleys for miles around. Being close to the equator, it is hot and humid all year. By car or bus, the town is a drive of at least three hours' duration from the nearest airports of Padang or Medan. There is only one international hotel, managed by Novotel, and built in a joint venture with the Indonesian government which included a conference facility. There are several 'backpacker' hotels and other accommodation in the town. Despite the problems of access, Bukittingi experiences tourism visits from the many backpackers who find their way across Sumatra via service buses and from a number of conference and convention delegates who attend the recently-constructed conference centre. Alongside the scenery, unique Sumatran architecture and the celebrated local cuisine, the town offers two main visitor attractions. The first of these is the weekly market, a magnet for all tourists and many locals who are present on a Saturday. The second is the 'Lepong Japang' – a complex of tunnels constructed using slave labour during the occupation of the town by the Japanese in the Second World War.

The Lepong Japang is located close to the centre of the town within a small area of urban parkland for which a modest entry fee is levied – mainly because of the spectacular views afforded from the park. The practice of erecting a fence around a desirable or famous vista and charging an entry fee to those who wish to enjoy the scene is common in Sumatra. At the entry to the park there is a small wooden sign which simply announces the Lepong Japang in Bahasa (the language of Indonesia). No other announcement of the presence, significance or availability of the tunnel is evident anywhere in Bukittingi.

The tunnels are reached via a rough and uneven path which leads to the main entrance where a number of 'guides' sit awaiting business. There is a small charge to enter the tunnels and, for a larger payment, one of the guides will accompany visitors. Upon payment, these guides give their version of the history of the tunnels, in Bahasa, illustrating this by running their fingers along an elementary coloured and relief map of the maze of tunnels cut into the wall-face of the entrance. Thereafter, visitors follow the guide into the tunnels via an immediate drop of more than 120 steep stairs cut into the rock. Lighting is poor and the guide constantly warns the party to stay with him and not to wander into the many chambers opening to left and right which, he says, are unexplored and possibly dangerous. As he proceeds, he continues his commentary in Bahasa, showing where the Japanese military had its command post, billets, kitchens, etc. At one point, in the kitchens, he indicates a large hole in the floor which is, apparently, a sheer drop of several hundred feet into a subterranean river below. This, he tells us, was the means by which disposal of the casualties of tunnel building was effected. His commentary suggests that the tunnelling process was kept secret from the town and that the labour was imported from elsewhere. Unsurprisingly, many died, and disposal without discovery by locals was a priority for the occupying army – hence the use of this hole. It is unclear how many people died in the construction of these tunnels as no records were kept. The 'official' figure, according to the guide, is 'hundreds of thousands'. Visitors can proceed in a round trip through the tunnels or be taken to the (formerly) secret back gate opening onto a narrow mountain road. Located at this back gate is an unkempt memorial to the victims of the Japanese occupation.

There are no maps, guidebooks or souvenirs at this stark and quite remote site. The only concession to interpretation other than the guides, who are effectively enterprising locals who see an opportunity to make a few rupiah from tourists, are four coin-in-the-slot machines deep in the tunnel complex which deliver a short, deadpan recital of the tunnels in Bahasa. These tunnels at Bukittingi are interesting as much for the atrocity which they portray as for the manner in which these events are offered and interpreted to visitors.

It is clear from a number of sources that tourist interest in recent death, disaster and atrocity is a growing phenomenon in the late twentieth and early twenty-first centuries and that theorists have both noticed and attempted to understand it. Rojek (1993a) in discussing what he calls 'fatal attractions' offers the observations that such sites have become modern pilgrimage sites. John Urry (1990) discusses the nature of the Gestapo Museum in Berlin within the context of Foucault's 'gaze'. Using these as a starting point for our fieldwork, we have studied a number of sites (Foley and Lennon, 1995a, 1995b, 1996, 1997), in the course of a fieldwork programme which has extended across the world. In labelling some of these phenomena as 'Dark Tourism' we intend to signify a fundamental shift in the way in which death, disaster and atrocity are being handled by those who offer associated tourism 'products'. In particular, we aim to show that 'dark tourism' is both a product of the circumstances of the late modern world and a significant influence upon these circumstances. Moreover, the politics, economics, sociologies and technologies of the contemporary world are as much important factors in the events upon which this dark tourism is focused as they are central to the selection and interpretation of sites and events which become tourism products.

Several commentators view pilgrimage as one of the earliest forms of tourism (Vellas and Becherel, 1995; Lickorish and Jenkins, 1997). This pilgrimage is often (but not only) associated with the death of individuals or groups, mainly in circumstances which are associated with the violent and the untimely. Equally, these deaths tend to have a religious or ideological significance which transcends the event itself to provide meaning to a group of people. Generally, it has been elements of those who attribute significance to the events who have comprised the pilgrims, who have visited either the site of the deed or the site of the burial or both. Such acts of remembrance, sometimes acquiring greater significance at certain times of the year, are a feature of the memorialization of death, whether untimely or not, in many societies. In societies based upon Judaeo-Christian beliefs, the dead are often buried in sites designated for this purpose and memorialized via a headstone, or more obtrusive device, above or around the point of burial. Whatever the religious and social significance of these practices, the outcome is to leave a 'permanent' site which those who wish can visit, knowing that the corpse of the individual to be remembered is close by. Practices associated with death and remembrance are highly ritualized in almost all societies where there is a belief system based upon the separation of body and soul and an afterlife or reincarnation, whether or not a 'final resting place' for the corporeal remains is designated. Sudnow (1967) and more recently Walter (1996) have pointed to the increasing 'industrialization' of death in the late twentieth century in some cultures where businesses associated with all aspects of a process that includes hardware, real estate and funeral or, even, cryogenic services have arisen, some global in their scope.

Pilgrimage has a religious or, at least, mystical significance – sometimes mandatory as a requirement of religious adherence – which contains elements of both a personal physical as well as often a psychological journey for participants. Sometimes this can be associated with attaining social and/or economic standing and with a collective affirmation of values. Although by no means the earliest record of a pilgrimage, whether real or fictional, Geoffrey Chaucer's *Canterbury Tales*, themselves a product of an emergent new reprographical technology, arose from the journey of a group of people to the death site of Thomas à Becket at Canterbury Cathedral.

Tourism to battle sites, to the graves of the famous, the infamous and the merely affluent and to the locations of infamous deeds is by no means a phenomenon associated with the modern world (Seaton, 1996). Visiting sites which could be said to be connected in some way to death (e.g. murder sites, death sites, battlefields, cemeteries, mausoleums, churchyards, the former homes of now-dead celebrities) is a significant part of tourist experiences in many societies. There is, however, little research available on the significance that such visits have to those who make them. It is not reasonable to simply assume that a death site which may be part of a comfort stop on a coach tour itinerary is any less significant for an individual than a trip undertaken to a remote or distant shrine. However, it is clear that one involves considerably more personal commitment, intention and inconvenience than the other. Is it possible that some death sites have become the locations (or, even, excuses) for service industries supplying conveniently-spaced watering-holes, lavatories and retail outlets designed to intervene in the journeys made by visitors through our heritages and landscapes?

The relative status of these death sites suggests that this proposition can, at most, only partly hold. The sites belonging to the Commonwealth War Graves Commission (CWGC) throughout Belgium and northern France, for example, appear both far less commercialized and far more politically significant than the Graceland home of Elvis Presley. Yet elements of both of these possess a resonance in popular culture which cannot be discerned within, say, the site of the Battle of Hastings – an event which was indubitably politically significant – located in a part of Kent which is well used to providing tourist services.

Some have argued that, through its presentation, whether real or fictional, in popular culture, death has become a commodity for consumption in a global communications market (Palmer, 1993). These arguments have often proceeded from the idea that the rituals surrounding death in 'ordinary' circumstances in Western cultures have somehow become 'privatized', i.e. that they have ceased to be a matter for public shows of grief among whole communities but, rather, mourning and observance of death rituals have become a matter for immediate families and friends of the deceased or, more likely, the relatives of the deceased. Clearly, a number of social variables have contributed to this change in the way that death is handled: presumably the greater longevity of populations, the geographical fragmentation of families, the growth in the number of cremations compared to burials, the increase in payments of death benefits by insurance companies, multi-culturalism and the practices of undertakers and others involved in catering for funeral ceremony, all will have had their effects. However, it can also be argued that via news media and popular televized fiction, many face the issues of death on a regular, perhaps daily, basis. It is disputed whether these kinds of experiences can be considered to accurately reflect the emotions and traumas of sudden or unexpected death but it is, nevertheless, likely that most viewers of television, readers of fiction and cinema-goers will have had an experience of death via replication. In the case of global news media, deaths across the entire planet can be consumed in the living rooms of the Western world. Some of these deaths may stimulate responses such as 'Live Aid' while others, such as those illustrated via reconnaissance footage shown during the Gulf War, may seem remote and 'unreal' – amounting to 'collateral damage' in the words of contemporary press conferences. These multiple 'real' deaths are underscored by the 'real' deaths of single, sometimes iconic, individuals whose lives of celebrity have become part of the media landscape inhabited by many. The deaths of these individuals offer opportunities for media presentation of the events, circumstances and minutiae of the death itself, complete with theories, eye-witness testimony, speculations and 'expert' analysis as part of the package. Events as diverse in place and time as the assassination of John Kennedy and the death of Diana, Princess of Wales, provide the touchstones for this form of media commodity. Finally, televised and cinematic presentations put characters in tragic, deadly or dangerous circumstances – either as 'real' individuals (e.g. the characters in the film *Schindler's List*) or as fictionalized characters operating within the context of 'real' events (e.g. the characters in the film *Titanic*). These deaths and disasters, too, are consumed precisely for the danger in which characters are placed and in which some are expected to die.

It is argued that it is unreasonable to separate the viewing public which assimilates these media commodities and those who seek tourism experiences. No demographic point is being made here, it is simply argued to be axiomatic that the vast majority of those consuming tourism experiences will be familiar with many of these global media events. It is more difficult to ascertain the impact of these commodified deaths upon the psychology of individuals, but it seems at least reasonable to expect that any tourism product designed around such an event will at least enjoy the benefit of 'familiarity'. This 'familiarity' is not present at Bukittingi, for example. While, on the one hand, the events of the Japanese occupation appear to have led to multiple deaths and must surely rate as crimes against humanity, on the other, these events are little known outwith the immediate area and have certainly not formed the backdrop to a film, book or television drama. In short, they have not been commodified for Western media consumption.

Tourism in the modern world

Tourism as a form of educative enterprise is strongly associated with the key principles of modernity (Burkart and Medlik, 1981; Cooper *et al.*, 1993). Grounded in the 'grand tour' of Europe as undertaken by the rich and powerful of the late seventeenth century and popularized in the excursions of Thomas Cook in the mid-nineteenth century, moving to another place, or from place to place, for the purposes of leisure in the Aristotelian sense, an educative pursuit (Parker, 1976) or for the purposes of recreation (offsetting the effects of industrial and urban squalor) is principally an issue of personal development and improvement. These improvements came, not surprisingly, in the wake of marketing efforts by industrial corporations (e.g. Thomas Cook) and the infrastructural developments associated with industrialization across (mainly) Europe and the USA.

Defining elements of 'modern' tourism have included ideas of universalism, classification and the liberal democratic state. The wealth and freedom to travel and the education to benefit from the experience are facets of late industrialism which arose in the context of universal suffrage, the spread of education and the onset of a tourism industry which encompassed aspects of travel, accommodation and attractions. In some of its earliest explicit support for the tourism industries of Europe, the EEC (as was) expressed it as a matter of mutual cultural exchange leading to common understandings and making war less likely in the future (Wilson and Van der Dussen, 1993; Waites, 1993). These cultural exchanges were equally likely to take place at a Mediterranean resort or in the Louvre. In this sense all tourism is cultural tourism (Richards, 1995) as it is virtually impossible to travel to another culture without experiencing some of its effects and products. The growth of tourism to Europe and, subsequently, to the USA has arisen simultaneously with a growth in travel opportunities and global communications. As we have visited other places, we have come to know more about the day-to-day life of these and other nations. Equally, it has become more likely that media organizations will have a correspondent in many nation-states and major cities and that some of these destinations will be more likely to see economic benefits from allowing studios to make films on location. If a diplomatic, political, economic or technological crisis develops in any part of the world, it is likely that it will make it onto the Western news media with 'live' pictures within a matter of hours.

The technologies which have combined to make this collapsing of time and space in news reporting possible have been wrought in the outcomes of the project of modernity and have been conceived largely within living memory. Critical elements of the ability to experience news from abroad have included the ability to take and process photographs, the ability to transfer these and associated text to another place, the ability to record sound and cinematic motion (Lumière brothers, 1896), the invention of radio and television and the launching of communications satellites. (In attempting to locate the concept of 'dark tourism' in a temporal context, it is clear to us that our interest does not extend beyond the congruence of at least some of these inventions.)Although there were many photographs and front-line reports returned from the Crimean and the American Civil Wars, for example, it is clear that the events of these conflicts were relatively divorced from the day-to-day lives of all but those directly affected. In part, this was due to the nature of these conflicts themselves. A more likely candidate, and one from 'living memory' for the earliest event which could stimulate 'dark tourism' is the First World War, both due to the way in which all households in all of the countries involved were affected and due to the way in which the conflict was reported and the way in which (what purported to be) 'live' film from the Battle of the Somme, and other battles, was shown in British cinemas. The First World War graphically demonstrated the consequences of modernity to populations using the technology of modernity to achieve its effect. One slightly earlier event, the sinking of RMS *Titanic* in 1912, offers similar analytical possibilities (Deuchar, 1996) and this has been (relatively arbitrarily) selected as the chronological starting point for 'dark tourism'. The *Titanic* is particularly apt not only because of the questions its sinking raised about technological 'progress' but also because it receded into relative obscurity until the 1958 film *A Night to Remember*, revisited awareness of some of the social circumstances of 1912 and the issue of how close the possibility of rescue had been. Similar revisits to the First World War had harnessed another motif of modernity, critical reflection, to propound the message about the savage and brutalizing effects of war; films such as *All Quiet on the Western Front, Gallipoli, Johnny Got His Gun* and, more recently, *The Trench*. Thus, these films purported to be, if not educative, then at least to inform and to warn. If they did not revise accounts of the war, they offered the possibility that accounts of it which might not be the 'official' version were possible and they offered a view that attempted to encourage future generations to consider armed conflict as a dangerous political route. In essence, these have been warnings about the consequences of planned death, often (but not always) on an industrial scale and scope (e.g. the Jewish Holocaust, the 'Killing Fields' of Cambodia) and derived from 'rational' principles. They have included scepticism of corporate politics and the (so-called) military–industrial complex.

If film has offered alternative, revised or more 'realistic' accounts of news events (e.g. *JFK*; *Apocalypse Now*; *Shoah*) throughout the twentieth century, then the events themselves have (apparently) come closer to us in space and time. In this sense, experiencing immediate news events, or critical reflection upon recent cataclysmic events, at, or near, home brings populations to the intersection between the global and the local. Can it be surprising that, when the opportunity presents itself to validate that global–local connection that so many decide to visit the sites of these deaths and disasters? Where tourism destinations encompass such 'celebrated' sites, should it be surprising that national and regional tourism bodies, voluntary groups and commercial businesses see opportunities to pursue their objectives?

For many of these organizations, a dilemma must be the extent to which a chronological distance can be effected between the event for which the site may be celebrated and the present. Of course, there are guides available to 'the most dangerous places on earth' and reports abound of those who visit these places during the moments of death, disaster and depravity – those in the vanguard of 'dark tourism'. But this is not mass tourism and it is not of much interest to those with economic, political or social aims. For these bodies, opportunities come later when the infrastructure has been repaired and when investment (often inward) is secured. Under these circumstances, a former concentration camp, battle site, assassination or killing site or the location of a disaster becomes a tourism resource to be exploited like any other. However, sensitivities abound and, although these may differ across cultures, there appears to be a certain 'global' format which accommodates mass tourism from the 'West'. It appears to be acceptable to visit death sites immediately following the events themselves to 'show respect' for the dead and to mourn. For example, the Oklahoma City bombing, the death of Diana, Princess of Wales, in a Paris underpass, and the massacre of schoolchildren in Dunblane, Scotland, brought spontaneous and public shows of grief and expressions of compassion at the sites themselves, often in the form of floral tributes. Thereafter, for some time it seems that it is unseemly to offer any kind of attempt to interpret events at the site itself – particularly if this involves what can be construed as 'exploitation'. It is likely that memorials will be erected and that these may be visited by those on a dedicated pilgrimage, those who are passing through and by the merely curious. What takes longer to be acceptable is any form of interpretation of the events – anything which could be said to be a touristic 'experience', however that experience may be intended. Yet, there appears to be a point at which this becomes acceptable. Examples of horrific events which are well embedded in mass consciousness through popular culture and media and which now are offered as part of cultural tourism experiences include several concentration camps in Poland and Germany, many of the battle sites of the First World War, Hiroshima, Pearl Harbor, sites of battles of the Vietnam War, the bridge over the River Kwai, the site of the massacre of civil rights marchers in Selma, Alabama, and Changi Gaol in Singapore. Individual deaths of political figures (e.g. John F. Kennedy, Martin Luther King), figures from popular culture (e.g. Elvis Presley, Marilyn Monroe, James Dean, River Phoenix), the victims of serial killers (e.g. Sharon Tate) and the sites of 'symbolic' deaths (e.g. Altamont Racetrack, California) all form parts of the tourism infrastructure in their respective locations.

Further problems arise when a cultural and/or touristic experience is offered at a site which has no direct connection with a 'dark' event, but seeks to exploit it for political, social or economic aims. A site such as the US Holocaust Memorial Museum in Washington, DC, with over 2.5 million visitors per annum has no direct spatial link with the Jewish Holocaust. Impressive though it undoubtedly is in its interpretation of events, its link is via the Jewish trust which conceived and funded it.

Similar problems arise of course for many museums which purport to interpret war and other such events. The various sites of the Imperial War Museum in the UK include a battle-cruiser permanently anchored in the Thames, a wartime airfield, the underground offices of Churchill's War Cabinet, but also a large museum in a former Victorian lunatic asylum. This museum contains much of the hardware of wars in the twentieth century with which Britain has been associated (with the notable exception of the 'troubles' in Northern Ireland, during our visit). It also contains two replicated environments – 'The Trench Experience', a presentation of conditions in a First World War trench on the Western Front, and the 'Blitz Experience', a presentation of conditions during the bombing of London during the Second World War, including the simulation of a bombing raid experienced from within an 'Anderson shelter'. Interesting though these are, especially for those studying these events in the UK schools National Curriculum, they can be said to both replicate and commodify the events which they seek to interpret.

Our argument is that 'dark tourism' is an intimation of post-modernity. We do not seek to enter any philosophical debates over the use of this term but, rather, aim to recognize the significant aspects of 'post-modernity' which are broadly taken to represent its main features. If these features amount to late capitalism, or late modernity, then so be it. The critical features apparent in the phenomena are, first, that global communication technologies play a major part in creating the initial interest (especially in exploring the territory between the global and the local, thereby introducing a collapse of space and time); second, that the objects of dark tourism themselves appear to introduce anxiety and doubt about the project of modernity (e.g. the use of 'rational planning' and technological innovation to undertake the Jewish Holocaust, the industrial scale of death in several wars this century, the failure of 'infallible' science and technology at the sinking of the *Titanic*, the impact upon liberal democracy of assassinations such as those of Kennedy or King, the contradictions apparent in the Cold War tensions and the resolution of these in the progress, rationality and associated so-called meta-narratives; third, the educative elements of sites are accompanied by elements of commodification and a commercial ethic which (whether explicit or implicit) accepts that visitation (whether purposive or incidental) is an opportunity to develop a tourism product.

Battle, and other, sites of events (broadly) prior to the start of the twentieth century continue to be the subject of visitor interest, as they have been over the centuries since the particular events which they hosted took place. We do not disagree that these sites are hosts to tourism, or even that films, novels and television do not stimulate interest in them (witness the increase in visits to sites of the Scottish Wars of Independence since the release of the film *Braveheart*, 1996) or that commodification and commercialization are not common. However, these do not qualify as 'dark tourism' within our analysis for two main reasons. First, there is the simple matter of chronological distance. These events did not take place within the memories of those still alive to validate them. Second, the events of ancient and medieval battles, etc., do not posit questions, or introduce anxiety and doubt about, modernity and its consequences. It is this particular element of the commodification of anxiety and doubt within interpretations offered and the design of the sites as both products and experiences (including merchandising and revenue generation) that introduces 'dark tourism'.

CHAPTER TWO

Instances of Dark Tourism

Changi Gaol in Singapore was the site of many atrocities perpetrated upon British and other Allied soldiers during the Second World War. It contained many prisoners who would be compelled to work on the so-called 'death railway' and the bridge over the River Kwai project. Presently, Changi continues its function as a gaol, serving the state of Singapore – its wartime function having been largely forgotten until pressure from groups of Allied war veterans and their families wishing to return to the site found little to commemorate the events of the Japanese occupation. This pressure resulted in the allocation of a small building (in fact, the former prison officers' social club) and the dedication of a small, open-air, wooden chapel upon a piece of land immediately adjoining the huge walls and gates of the current gaol. Under the watchtowers of Singapore's main prison, visitors can visit a small interpretative centre in the former social club and may pay their respects at the chapel. The chapel is interesting because of the vehemence of some of the messages left behind upon the notice board – this being the only site visited in the course of the fieldwork where such strong feelings of anger were witnessed, albeit in written form. Certainly intended as a place of peace, this chapel has become a focus for the strong feelings about some of the deeds of Imperial Japan during the Second World War and the failure of the British and other governments to secure what some see as an adequate apology or reparation for sufferings caused. The interpretation centre alongside the chapel offers contemporary drawings and accounts from former inmates as well as some interpretation of the events of the occupation of Singapore. Items on sale include some lurid contemporary 'underground' cartoons featuring gross stereotypes of Japanese soldiers and quasi-pornographic images representing their violent and cruel behaviour. The reactions at the chapel and the books on sale are certainly unusual among the sites of death and suffering visited, where a spirit of reconciliation at least purported to be on offer.

These elements of Changi are far removed from the 'English country garden' ambience of the cemeteries of the Commonwealth War Graves Commission. Spread throughout the world, these are the final resting places of Commonwealth soldiers who have died in combat since (and including) the First World War. The graves at these sites are of white Portland stone and a series of stylized memorials are replicated at all sites, including the visitors' book, Cenotaph and crucified sword. The overall feeling is one of peace, tranquillity and restraint, wherever these sites are. The upkeep of the sites is met via taxation which covers the costs of local employees who tend the sites. In contrast, German war graves of the twentieth century are tended by young German volunteers who spend short periods with responsibilities at a site. Cemeteries, which have often been consolidated from a number of sites into one, are far darker in their aspect, often under the shade of a tree canopy and with rough-hewn or plaque grave markings in dark stone, accompanied by Teutonic figures in the common memorial areas. Yet further contrasts are offered by the manner of remembrance offered for US soldiers who died in Europe and Asia during the twentieth century. War graves exist at the sites of a number of battles, or close by, often offering Graeco-Roman heroic imagery in the statues and images used and with 'reflecting pools' and galleries. Commonly, these sites are set out as 'parklands', with graves marked as white stone crosses or Stars of David. Families of US soldiers who die abroad have the right of repatriation of the bodies. The range of remembrance in the US itself is best epitomized by Maya Ling's design for the Vietnam War Memorial (a black polished stone crescent, tapering at each end and upon which the names of all fatalities are etched) on the one hand, and the Korean War Memorial (bronze 'realist' statues of a platoon moving heavily through a landscape), both in Washington, DC.

In grave and remembrance sites such as those mentioned above, visitation is unlikely to fall within the category to which we assign the term dark tourism. Visits, whether by friends and relatives of the dead or by those with other motives, can be broadly considered under similar

1   *Vietnam Vets Memorial, Washington*

2   *Korean Vets Memorial, Washington*

categories to pilgrimage. Nevertheless, the US Vietnam War Memorial, both in its design and in the messages and artefacts left behind by visitors, suggests an element of anxiety and doubt, both national and personal, about the meaning and conduct of this war for 'the world's greatest democracy'. Clearly, it is far less triumphalist than the war grave sites at, say, Omaha Beach in Normandy or the 'Punch Bowl' in Honolulu, Hawaii. Similarly, the images offered at the Korean War Memorial close by are grim but realistic, a product, it seems, of the period of reflection since the events themselves.

Global communication technologies

As suggested earlier, our thesis is that global communication technologies are inherent in both the events which are associated with a dark tourism product and are present in the representation of the events for visitors at the site itself. Perhaps the most celebrated instance of this can be seen in the way in which the assassination of John F. Kennedy in 1963 captured consciousness world-wide and continues to maintain an interest for many. Although it will be argued later that Kennedy's death and its aftermath are symptomatic of anxieties and doubts about liberal democratic government (in the same way as the Vietnam War, for example), here we wish to touch upon the impact of global communication technologies upon public awareness and perception of events, bringing these 'into our living-rooms'.

The death of Kennedy was the first major news event in which global communication technologies were able to be harnessed in urgency to report momentous events almost simultaneously throughout much of the world. Television broadcasts were interrupted across the globe to break the news. In the USA, coverage took precedence over scheduled programming and announcers (e.g. the famous scenes of Walter Cronkite appearing to weep on CBS) extemporized on camera as news changed and events unfolded. Subsequently, the alleged assassin, Lee Harvey Oswald, was himself shot during a live television broadcast from outside a jail in Dallas, Texas. The coverage of Kennedy's state funeral again led to the replacement of scheduled programming, this time beyond the USA, and timeless images of the grieving widow, the saluting young son, the riderless horse and the 'eternal flame' from Washington, DC, and Arlington, Virginia, entered the public consciousness via television coverage as (virtually) the blueprint for such coverage (cf. the death, aftermath and funeral of Diana, Princess of Wales) was written by television companies. In this respect, television mediated in the experience of the death of Kennedy for millions across the globe. Having created the effect, the circumstances surrounding the death and associated events continued to offer communications media the opportunity to maintain public interest in Kennedy – the assassination of Robert Kennedy, the incident at Chappaquidick, the Warren Commission and the revelation of the existence of Abraham Zappruder's cine film of the actual moments of the assassination in Dallas all amounted to moments of communication. Subsequently, a number of books and films (for further discussion, see Chapter 6) maintained the momentum, principally purveying various degrees of conspiracy theories connected with Kennedy's death. Perhaps the greatest irony is that Kennedy himself had been seen as a consummate user of televisual media to transmit political messages. Of course, the extent of media coverage received by Kennedy in life and in death have enabled a number of sites to construct interpretations of his death, and celebrations of his life using just these representations of the man. Sites associated with John F. Kennedy are dealt with in more detail in Chapter 6.

It has been argued that the sinking of the *Titanic* was the first, real, global event, due to its impact upon news media worldwide. Of course, the immediate impact available due to technologies of the 1960s was not available in 1912, but newspaper reports appeared quickly and newsreel companies filmed survivors being landed in the USA, sending these back to cinema audiences throughout Europe and the Americas. If Kennedy's assassination and its aftermath were a practical illustration of 'shrinking' time and space in the late twentieth century, the sinking of the 'unsinkable' *Titanic* equally illustrated the technological possibilities of global communications in its time – and with similar effects in terms of the introduction of doubts and anxieties about the 'progress' in which so much faith had been placed in the early part of the century, in this case, technological and scientific improvement. However, the largest impact made by global communication technologies upon consciousness of the *Titanic* and its sinking came with the 1958 film *A Night to Remember*, which, effectively, turned the relatively impersonal and largely forgotten sinking into a series of individual 'stories' of fictional characters upon the vessel. By the time of the 1998 film, *Titanic*, the stories of individuals and the doomed ship had melded into one text and charter companies were offering Titanic Cruises in which meals identical to those served and music identical to that played on the *Titanic* were offered during a visit to the precise spot where the ship lies (when a religious service of remembrance was carried out). Such certainties about the circumstances of the liner and the details of the passage can be replicated because of marine technology which has been able both to find the ship and raise artefacts from it, some of which were put on display at the National Maritime Museum in Greenwich, UK. As part of that exhibition, the curator's appearance on a television programme to discuss the ethics of the exhibition with a grandchild of a survivor was shown on a perpetual video loop. Further analysis of the *Titanic* exhibition, which placed as heavy reliance upon interpreting the technology used to raise artefacts as to the artefacts themselves is given in a paper by the curator himself (Deuchar, 1996). A similar recourse to technological matters when interpreting a 'difficult' event for exhibition is that of the 'Enola Gay' exhibition at the Smithsonian Air and Space Museum, Washington, DC. The aircraft 'Enola Gay' dropped the first atomic bomb on the Japanese city of Hiroshima in 1945. More or less since then, debate has raged over whether the decision to drop the bomb and the action of doing it were 'justified' according to rational criteria (essentially, whether it saved lives which would have been lost by service personnel fighting through the Pacific, island by island, or whether the mass killing of civilians and the unleashing of the technology itself could ever be justified). Although housed relatively uncontroversially for a long period in New Mexico, the proposed removal of 'Enola Gay' to Washington introduced considerable debate in the press over whether this was desirable and of how the events of Hiroshima should be interpreted in the exhibition. The Smithsonian, which is free to enter, issues further free, numbered tickets to the 'Enola Gay' exhibition and operates a level of security which is unusual in a US museum (removal of bags, etc., prior to entry). The exhibit itself amounts to the front portion of the aircraft, the remainder being restored elsewhere for subsequent display, and the interpretation, while devoting space and time to the events, contains a high proportion of material upon the, relatively uncontroversial, techniques of restoration which will be used.

Both Checkpoint Charlie and the Berlin Wall itself came to symbolize, through news media and popular fiction (whether in books, television or film), the Cold War and the division of ideologies in Europe. Although the eventual 'fall of the Wall' came to be dubbed a post-modern motif and suggested that the meta-narrative of Marxism–Leninism had died, more important to this portion of the argument is the representation of the Berlin Wall and its media significance. The Wall and Checkpoint Charlie (the main crossing point and border control) are interpreted for visitors to Berlin in the Checkpoint Charlie Museum, which locates the struggle of those attempting to either escape or survive under oppression in East Germany within a global context of media and other images from 'equivalent' circumstances in the twentieth century (e.g. civil rights in the USA, the Indian sub-continent during Gandhi's campaigns, South Africa under apartheid, etc.). Thus this museum represents political struggle via media images. Media images at the fall of the Wall are equally powerful, with pictures being relayed across the world as they happened (representing considerable collapse of time and space since the Kennedy assassination and its *post-hoc* coverage of the actual event) and reporters triumphantly entering television studios with broken fragments of concrete. Subsequently, of course, portions of the Wall have been exported throughout the world (e.g. the piece outside the Imperial War Museum in London) and there were even proposals to replicate a section of the wall, including a border post, as an 'attraction' in Florida.

A by-product of the 'peace dividend' following the end of the Cold War has been the sale of British 'bunkers', originally intended to house the government in the event of a nuclear war. At least two of these (one in England and one in Scotland) have become tourism products ('Based just 20 miles from central London this bunker was one of Britain's best kept secrets and now it is open to you!') dedicated to presenting the technologies and effects of nuclear holocaust (e.g. replicated effects of a direct hit close by, etc.). Ambivalence about the morality of a nuclear holocaust is present in the relatively limited interpretation of the political ramifications of global holocaust (other than the brochure's suggestion that government ministers, 'possibly including the Prime Minister' could have been located at these sites) or what the aftermath would be like and a greater concentration upon the technology of the bunker's construction and operating constraints, together with the attempts taken to maintain the 'secret' underground.

Final consideration needs to be given to situations where reality and representation are inconsistent with each other. The British television series *Colditz* of the 1970s followed a 1955 film of the same name, both based loosely upon the recounted attempts of a British officer to escape from an 'escape-proof' German prisoner of war camp housed in a castle. Although several cruelties were inflicted upon the officers (persistent escapees from other camps) located in the camp, it seems that suffering may not have been as great there as in, say, concentration camps or even other prisoner of war camps. Nevertheless, the themes of war, escape, Nazism and seemingly impossible odds which required ingenuity-stretching plans for escape proved a heady mixture for cinema and television audiences. In fact, neither the castle represented in the film nor that shown over the opening credits of the television series are Colditz Castle. The 'real' castle and the small town which bears its name were, for many years, removed from maps by East German officials to discourage visitation from either previous inmates, their relatives or the merely curious. Colditz tourist information centre now offers a modest tour of the castle and some of the celebrated sites, including tunnels started by Allied prisoners but discovered by their captors. Impressively located upon a high rock, the castle is an imposing sight, but manifestly not that of the various media representations. Similar remarks can, of course, be made about the bridge over the River Kwai, which is of steel construction and wholly unlike the bridge built by Allied prisoners in the film of the same name.

Global communication technologies have shaped perceptions of what are the significant sites in the political history of the twentieth century. Undoubtedly some sites may possess significance, but have not received attention from cinematic or televisual media, the principal communicators of these messages to individuals worldwide. Whether Tiananmen Square or Watergate, sites become invested with significance arising from events associated with them. Interestingly, neither of these sites have, to date, sought to harness the notoriety delivered by global media into a tourism product – tempting speculation into why some sites become sites of dark tourism and some do not (see below). Whatever, dark tourism sites reflect the role of these media in their individual significance by harnessing the artefacts, texts and power of the media in representing the events themselves as part of a product for visitors, thereby becoming self-referential in their representations but not always deconstructing the events themselves. A significant exception to this principle is the Museum of Tolerance in Los Angeles, which is attached to the Simon Wiesenthal Center. This museum contains few original 'objects' as its focus, rather, it uses a series of media images and communications technologies to both represent intolerances, such as racism, and to expose the individual intolerances of visitors themselves. Although strongly associated with the Jewish Holocaust and the monitoring of right-wing political groups, the theme of the museum is intolerance generally, with a view to encouraging participation by users which, in turn, leads to critical reflection upon personal values and behaviours. While not located upon a site of atrocity itself, it uses its combined database and information communication technologies to offer both a global (the starting point for analysis is Turkish persecution of Armenians in 1915) and local (e.g. the 'Rodney King' affair) perspective within a multi-ethnic, multi-cultural city. Few sites visited in the course of this research sought to actively engage with personal anxieties and doubts in such an overt and political manner.

The next section considers a number of sites where the self-referentiality of dark tourism sites introduces anxieties and doubts (whether explicitly or implicitly) about the key tenets of the project of modernity such as progress, rationality, science, technology, industrialization and liberal democracy.

Anxiety, doubt and incredulity towards meta-narratives

The project of modernity has, according to some, raised rationality, progress and the general shift to prominence over anxiety, doubt and the particular. Yet modernity and its industrialized, rationally planned and politically 'mature' circumstances have clearly had their ambivalences, ambiguities and anxieties, e.g. rationally planned and industrially delivered death during the Nazi's (so-called) Final Solution, the terms themselves evoking the language of bureaucracy, planning and problem-solving applied to corporate strategies. Within the project of modernity, events such as this should be morally inconceivable, politically impossible and economically unsustainable. Yet these events happen and (some) reach public consciousness, whether via news, cinematic or other media. Events or circumstances which fit this profile of ambiguity and ambivalence include the dropping of atomic bombs on Hiroshima and Nagasaki in 1945, the fire-bombing of Dresden in 1945 and the war of attrition fought in trenches across France and Belgium between 1914 and 1918. All of these events required technologies, planning approaches and military–industrial complexes to enable them to happen – instances of the project of modernity which, apparently, were being used in ways which extended rationality beyond humanism, i.e in which human casualties were viewed as 'collateral damage' (or some such term) on the route towards a 'greater goal'.

No particular political point is being made here – simply that the artefacts and attitudes of modernity have reached a stage of ambivalence and ambiguity which continues to be present in some public consciousnesses. Similar outcomes of modernity which have apparently introduced anxiety into events and circumstances could be said to be the much publicized and often fictionalized growth of 'organized' crime in the USA on rational economic scales and using behavioural and other models or sytems of management. The apparent surprise of many US citizens (including, it seems, Eisenhower himself) and the wider media of liberal USA in 1958 to find that black children were being excluded from the Central High School in Little Rock, Arkansas, was the opening salvo in what could euphemistically be called a debate upon the extent to which it was possible to rationalize the system of 'Jim Crow' in some of the southern states. To find forms of racism, intimidation and disenfranchisement, both overt and institutionalized, within the boundaries of the (apparently) shining meritocratic, pluralistic and democratic USA was yet another anxiety over the capabilities of modernity to deliver the kind of political progress measured by the ideals of the French Revolution – liberty, equality and fraternity.

Thus, our second major consideration of instances of dark tourism explores the way in which some sites which have explored the anxieties and doubts inherent in modernity have become tourism venues (and some have not), how these sites have been managed and the manner in which events associated with them have been 'staged'. It is not our contention that these sites necessarily have tourism as their sole, or even, primary object (although some have). Nevertheless, by any accepted definition of the term 'tourism', these sites accommodate 'tourists' and contribute tourism revenues to local, and national, economies. We do not suggest that visitors attend with the sole intention of receiving entertainment, amusement or enjoyment (even where their visit is wholly touristic) or the significant quantities of visitors who see these venues as the sole, or main, reason for their trip (although, again and in certain circumstances, some do). Thus, we do not see something as simple as a lucrative niche market of 'dark tourists' who can be segmented by carriers and package holiday companies – in essence, our approach to understanding the phenomena suggests that those who visit such sites as 'specialists', whether seeking the location of their relatives' sufferings or pursuing the technology of tank warfare or revisiting regimental glories, or whatever, are not a crucial, or even important, part of dark tourism. It is those who visit due to serendipity, the itinerary of tour companies or the merely curious who happen to be in the vicinity who are, for us, the basis of dark tourism. To those, the importance of merchandising (and, possibly, personal or authoritative recommendation) to secure an 'impulse purchase' or visit becomes central to the product involved. It would be interesting to see research conducted among this group by others with interests in the psychology of consumption.

Sites associated with Nazism and the Jewish Holocaust

Although there is some greater detail provided below, it is worth reviewing some of the issues which arise in the examination of sites associated with the Jewish Holocaust as tourism venues. Many sites are located behind what became known as the 'Iron Curtain' in the language of the Cold War. These received the interpretation offered by Marxist–Leninist regimes during the post-war period and visits were, essentially, a compulsory element of school curricula and 'controlled' tourism under such regimes. Interpretation of this sort could still be witnessed at Sachsenhausen outside Berlin (and in the former 'East') during our fieldwork and amounted to a glorification of the triumph of the 'anti-Fascist' forces over the evils of racism, etc. The style of interpretation on display at Sachsenhausen, while changing slowly, demonstrated many features of museum and heritage site practice throughout Europe and the USA during the late 1960s onwards, namely, a central gallery with lots of information presented on boards together with artefacts behind glass and some illustrations of what had happened, allowing for some 'artistic' licence. Of course, memorials were erected to the dead and the actual locations of the death sites themselves (in this case, a pit in which victims were shot) tended to retain the minimum of interpretation. The crypt in which corpses were kept and the adjoining hospital block, with a hint of experimentation upon human subjects in its interpretation, also imparted relatively minimal information to visitors, despite their chilling aspect. What is most interesting about this site is the extent to which later uses of the camp, following the end of the Second World War, are barely mentioned (or, at least, not in the presentation prepared prior to unification). The camp, and an adjoining one in which Allied prisoners of war were kept, were a convenient detention centre for political dissidents opposed to the status quo, being close to Berlin, and were used for this purpose for some time into the 1950s by the East German authorities. This information is available now at Sachsenhausen, but is far less obviously part of the 'story' than the Jewish connection. If political and (probably) medical–scientific meta-narratives are showing signs of ambivalence at Sachsenhausen, anxiety and doubt over their primacy reach some kind of crescendo in interpretations offered at both concentration camps located at Oswieczim (Auschwitz) in Poland – Auschwitz I and Auschwitz II, also known as Birkenau, a notorious death camp.

Auschwitz I was formerly a military barracks before being turned into a concentration camp by the Nazis. It is built of brick, predominantly, in individual huts and administration offices. Entry is free and guided tours are available. Many of the huts house exhibitions associated with individual nation–states affected by Nazism in the period 1938 to 1945. There are also some famously poignant interpretations of the extent of Nazi looting from those condemned to the camps – mounds of spectacles, shoes or artificial limbs encased behind glass remind the visitor of both the scale and scope of the theft as well as the effect at the individual and personal level. Exhibits such as these have become images to be replicated the world over in the interpretation of such sites. Particularly affecting is the almost complete absence of any commentary upon the objects themselves, thereby trusting the visitor to analyse and evaluate the exhibits (cf. the US Holocaust Memorial Museum, Washington, DC; the Museum of Human Genocide, Phnom Penh, Cambodia). Thus, in this particular situation at Auschwitz I, the visitor, whether Jew or gentile, is invited to doubt and to problematize the final solution in the general and the specific.

Although there are some ovens used to burn human remains at Auschwitz I, the greatest impact of the barbarity is achieved in the almost uninterpreted site of Birkenau, a short journey by bus. The gatehouse and adjoining railhead where 'selection' of those for slave labour and those who would be gassed was made are enduring images, probably as a result of several films, some documentary (e.g. Claude Lanzmann's *Shoah*) and some fictionalized versions of events (e.g. Steven Spielberg's *Schindler's List*). Combined with the bombed-out remains of the gas chambers and ovens, as well as the loneliness of the marshy site, again the opportunity to reflect without prescription or direction is offered. Clearly, there is an assumption or expectation from those who manage the site that visitors' conclusions can move in only one direction – but this is seldom, if ever, stated at the Auschwitz sites.

First World War sites in France and Belgium

A small sector of the tour industry has developed around visits to battlefield sites, the principal progenitors of which were Tonie and Valmai Holt, originators of Holt's Battlefield Tours. A key (but by no means, only) staple of this business has been bus tours starting at Victoria, in London, and taking in some of the principal battlefields of the First World War in Belgium and in France. Typically, these last for two days, usually over a weekend, and are aimed at the educated lay person with an interest in the First World War. There is no assumption of any specialist military or technical knowledge. The basic tour is a well-organized affair, encompassing almost military discipline upon customers to ensure efficient and effective embarkation and disembarkation of the bus and immediate realization if there is anyone missing from the tour complement. This tour is staffed by a bus driver, a guide who has expertise in the First World War, its sites and a knowledge of the layout of the cemeteries and an administrator. These are complemented by a number of audio tapes which are played at pre-arranged points and which include a 'voice-over' by Tonie Holt and some background sounds, both of the battlefield and of contemporary songs and accounts of the War (including that of the young Adolf Hitler). Visits include battle sites, such as the Somme, cemeteries of the Commonwealth War Graves Commission, local museums and a smaller number of cemeteries or memorials of other nations, including those of Germany, Canada and France. Particular attention is paid to certain individual graves, where these are of celebrated, or highly decorated (especially Victoria Crosses) or of otherwise remarkable individuals (e.g. young soldiers who were killed in action). The tone is, not unexpectedly, reverential with customers encouraged to bring items of remembrance and, where this is feasible, to lay flowers at the graves of family members, etc.

Commentary tends to take the part of the individual foot soldier or low-ranking officer at the front, whether Allied or Axis, and invites customers to infer that much of the blame for mass death and carnage is attributable to staff officers and military planners who, it is implied, failed to have any realistic analysis of the circumstances at the front and not to have understood the technology at their disposal.

Of course, although the conducted tour is itself a product, it depends upon a number of sites and venues to create its impact. Inevitably, due to their nature and purpose as well as their approach, these differ greatly in the way in which they portray war, death and remembrance.

The following chapters explore a range of sites from conception through to operation. Their history and the questions they raise about the nature of tourism at such 'attractions' are developed in the individual context.

CHAPTER THREE

The Third Reich and the Final Solution

Perhaps one of the most difficult aspects of coping with the phenomena that we have identified as dark tourism has been researching the interpretation and development of major sites of extermination and mass killing. The Holocaust and the jagged scars that it has left on the landscape of certain European countries in the form of concentration camp sites created moral ambiguities for issues of tourism development. Yet the fascination with dark aspects of human nature and history (Rojek, 1993a) is further echoed in the treatment of the Holocaust itself. The constant re-creation through film, texts and television of this era reminds us of the massive interest in this dark period of human history.

Mass killing sites, particularly those associated with the Jewish Holocaust, present major challenges for interpretation and invariably questions arise concerning the nature of motivation for visitors. The enormity of the systematic destruction of the Jewish people is beyond understanding and constitutes an enormous task in the sense of 'interpretation' and 'explanation'. The impossibility of language, images or art to deal with the Holocaust has already been the subject of critical debate (see, for example, Wiesel, 1968; Langer, 1975; Wyschogrod, 1975). The scope of the subject area is difficult to comprehend, yet visitation to concentration camps continues and such cities still receive visits from a huge range of ages and nationalities. Herein the nature of interpretation and documentation presents a potential danger for dealing with the Holocaust in artistic/moralistic terms; even documentary/historical approaches have inherent problems in dealing with this subject. As Steiner notes:

> Not only is the relevant material vast and intractable; it exercises a subtle, corrupting fascination. Bending too fixedly over hideousness, one feels queerly drawn. In some strange way the horror flatters attention . . . I am not sure whether anyone, however scrupulous, who spends time and imaginable resources on these dark places can, or, indeed, ought to leave them personally intact. (1971, pp. 30–1)

At the 'dark' sites of concentration camps and related locations in Europe tourists flock and read inscriptions, study site plans and purchase guidebooks. Estimated numbers of visitors per year for some of the more well-known sites are detailed in Table 3.1.

Table 3.1   Estimated numbers of visitors

Site	Visitors per year
Auschwitz (Poland)	750,000
Dachau (Germany)	900,000
The Anne Frank House (Amsterdam)	600,000
Majdanek (Poland)	300,000

(*Source*: Young, 1993)

These sites constitute attractions and they cannot simply be classified as 'Genocide Monuments' (Prentice, 1993) since a monument in this context conveys a different meaning and context (for further discussion on the nature and meaning of Holocaust monuments see Young, 1993).

These sites present major problems in interpretation that challenge current debates within literature on interpretation at heritage attractions (see, for example, Herbert, 1995). There are major problems for the language utilized in interpretation to adequately convey the horrors of the camps. Consequently, and because of the presence of historical records, visual representation is extensively used. Documentary evidence in the form of photographs is employed in sites of mass killing such as the Auschwitz–Birkenau complex at Oswieczem in Poland. Historical photographs and documentation of this nature have been central in transmitting the events of the Second World War. The visual heritage of the Nazi era is rich; the symbols of the SS, the swastika, the skeletal victims and the gates of Auschwitz. In taking the striking image of the gates and the railhead within Auschwitz II, a useful example of how central such a photographic image can be is provided. The visitor to the concentration camp looks at the documentary photograph showing guards and prisoners at the railhead (the past) to the current empty rails (the present), and in this way the camera has had the impact of what Barthes calls 'resurrection' (Barthes, 1981). The photographic image has the ability to transmit the reality of the death camps with a shock effect that words can rarely achieve. In this way the visitor can associate 'photographic time' and 'the past' with real time. However, as others have noted, the recurrent use of pictures of the victims and deportation trains can have the effect of an obsessive concentration with subject matter that can blur into unreality (see, for example, Lanzmann, 1995a). Indeed, there is an inherent danger in constant re-creation of the past, particularly if there is any attempt at stylization which can marginalize and indeed trivialize the enormity of the issues being dealt with.

A critical aspect of interpretation of Holocaust sites is dealing with what Steiner has called 'the time relation'. Here he is referring to the contemporary nature of Auschwitz in human history and how incomprehensible that is. It appears as 'the other planet' to the one in which we live our everyday lives:

Precisely at the same hour in which Mehring or Langer (victims of the camps) were being done to death, the overwhelming plurality of human beings, two miles away on Polish farms, five thousand miles away in New York, were sleeping or eating or going to a film or making love or worrying about the dentist. This is where my imagination balks. The two orders of simultaneous experience are so different, so irreconcilable to any common norm of human values, their co-existence is so hideous a paradox – Treblinka is both because some men have built it and almost all other men let it be . . . (Steiner, 1967, pp. 156–7)

This unreality and the problem of temporal and spatial affinity have been dealt with in a range of ways in film and media generally. The controversy surrounding the development of Spielberg's production of *Schindler's List* is illustrative of the problems faced. In this case, the film-maker had to recreate Auschwitz in the form of a film set on the outskirts of Krakow since he was not allowed to film within the camp. The film set construction itself became an attraction, which subsequently became known as 'The Schindler Tour'. This 'tour' continued for some two years after filming until it was dismantled. The film set had offered the visitor a conveniently located reconstruction of the concentration camp: a truly post-modern replication for the enormity of the real sprawling complex that is Auschwitz. However, the debate surrounding the film itself goes to the heart of this grim fascination with horror and atrocity and the dilemmas of sensitive interpretation. Spielberg not only re-created the camp as a film set, but his approach to *Schindler's List* was to re-create actual events, e.g. the deportation from the Krakow ghetto. This approach is not uncommon in works of film of the period (1950–85), this genre of reproducing 'actions' is dominant (for critical examinations see Avisar, 1988, and Insdorf, 1989). Yet the Schindler story of a German who saved 1,300 Jews can never communicate the enormity of the attempted wholesale extermination of the Jewish race. Rather, it operates within the confines of classic Hollywood narrative technique that is central to much popular cinema. 'Story' is necessary for effect and market appeal, as indeed are coherent chronological development and a clear 'plot'. The difficulty is that recounting the Holocaust in narrative form will limit and distort representation and visions of that reality. Reconstruction and replication are flawed in this context. The approach of Claude Lanzmann in the film *Shoah* is markedly different. It explores the legacy of the Final Solution by drawing the viewer into the debates of the original experience (Avisar, 1988). The work focuses on the death camps of Chelmno, Belzec, Majdanek, Sobibor, Treblinka and Auschwitz to reveal and document the genocide programme. It is not, however, an historical documentary. Rather, Lanzmann conveys the full amazement of holding in sight an item (a tower, gate, rails) that came from 'the other planet' with the use of extensive interviews with victims, bystanders, perpetrators and survivors. In using contemporary 'real time' and interviews while linking this with long screen takes of camp sites, trains, rails, etc., the connection between 'screen time' and 'real time' is established. In this way, rather than providing didactic, historical narrative or Hollywood stylized stories, the viewer is taken into the reality of the 'other planet' through this process of traumatic cultural shock. It ensures that the 'visitor' is able to appreciate the dreadful aspects of the past (the other planet) by dealing with its symptoms in the present. Lanzmann denies the viewer the dubious privilege of being a witness, rather, the viewer has to deal with more uncomfortable questions such as 'what does it mean to have witnessed it?' (Romney, 1995).

The problem of interpretation in concentration camps for visitors is not dissimilar. Orthodox museum display condones the feeling that one can stand back from the past and be 'educated' about it. Even relatively innovative museums such as the US Holocaust Memorial Museum, in Washington, DC, promote the idea of the past as 'another country' (Walsh, 1992). Simply put, the past is a place which is separate from the present, and which one travels to and visits via a combination of recreation and authentic elements. In contrast, the concentration camps themselves represent reality and here the task of the interpreter is vitally important in terms of allowing the public to differentiate between truth and falsity, reproduction and reality.

For some all interpretation remains ideological and this is evident in much of the interpretation of concentration camps in the former Communist states in Central/Eastern Europe. In many such countries, the Second World War was used as an ideological vehicle to expose the evil consequences of Fascism and to commemorate and celebrate Russia and/or Communism as the force of liberation. This type of political interpretation is still evidenced in concentration camps in the Czech Republic, the former East Germany and in Poland. In such cases the authority of interpretation becomes diluted and the displays as representations of the past lose the authority of their command over both time and space. The problems of interpretation are akin to the problems faced by the film-maker in this area. They are related to the difficulties of *representation* (creating a truthful account of the reality of Nazi rule) and *presentation* (paying tribute to and understanding the predicament of the victims and the context of genocide). The dilemma becomes avoidance of the potential for ideological distortions or deceptions.

The extreme alternative is non-interpretation and non-development of such sites. Literally, to adopt the call for silence made by Wiesel (1960) who claimed that 'Auschwitz negates any form of literature, as it defines all systems, all doctrines' (ibid., p. 7). Indeed, Steiner went further in arguing that it is best 'not to add the trivia of literary, sociological debate to the unspeakable' (1967, p. 163). Such thinking is both understandable and cogent yet silence brings with it the problem of displacement and may encourage future generations to forget or ignore the incidence of this terrible period of human history.

As Donat tells the listener in the name of Ignacy Schipper (the Warsaw historian):

> Everything depends on who transmits our testament to future generations, on who writes the history of this period. History is usually written by the victor . . . Should our murderers be victorious, should *they* write the history of this war, our destruction will be presented as one of the most beautiful pages of world history, and future generations will pay tribute to them as dauntless crusaders. Their every word will be taken for gospel. Or they may wipe out our memory altogether as if we had never existed, as if there had never been a Polish Jewry, a Ghetto in Warsaw, a Majdanek. Not even a dog will howl for us. (Donat, 1965, p. 6)

The analysis of such dark tourism sites in terms of their selection, interpretation, use of media and the understanding of motivation for visitation is important to develop an understanding of human behaviour and understanding events in the 'other past'. Such analysis is necessary for the appreciation of these sites. Yet, invariably, one is dealing with a subject so enormous that it threatens to overwhelm both media and language (Rosenfeld, 1980). Dealing with such a level of inhumanity can induce a sense of fatuity and even indecency. However, only through utilization of critical analysis and review of questions and interpretation and concomitant issues of taste and decency can one contribute to the debate and move towards 'understanding'. Only in this way can one move towards avoidance of compromising distortions or inadequate representations.

The challenge Germany faces with the legacy of its history is ever present. The return to Berlin of the national seat of government and the much debated 'museums' on the sites of former concentration camps serve to keep the past alive and part of a vibrant debate on history and interpretation. In the new Berlin 'dark' sites are evident and the Wall which previously divided the city has become a new retail commodity; boxed and sold to tourists seeking to touch an element of that past of division and danger.

Germany: new state, old preoccupations

In the heart of Berlin lie the foundations and remains of cells of the former SS and Gestapo headquarters – the *Gestapo Gelände* (Gestapo terrain). From 1933–9 increasingly the Nazi secret police became centrally located in the area of Wilhelmstrasse and Prinz-Albrecht-Strasse. Indeed, the former museums and state buildings became the nerve centre of the Nazi state security force. These buildings received sustained Allied bombing towards the end of the Second World War and many ruins of buildings were demolished by city authorities in the years of post-war reconstruction (Rürup, 1989, 1995).

However, this area has provoked massive controversy in terms of the most appropriate forms of 'interpretation'. The fear that any form of development might suggest a site for former SS or Nazi sympathizers to use for homage was voiced directly after the war. In response, the city authorities chose to demolish many of the buildings with a Nazi history. Such an approach literally obliterating memory has occurred more recently in the case of the site of Hitler's bunker. In late 1994 a *Fahrerbunker* (literally a smaller, less important refuge for minor Nazi functionaries) was located in the no-man's-land on the site of the former Berlin Wall. Unconnected to the main bunker (the *Führerbunker*) it served to catalyse debate about whether or not to preserve or destroy the entire site. The exact nature and location of the complex of tunnels and sanitoria are far from certain but interest in the site remains considerable. Indeed, this whole area has become a major real estate development opportunity, offering a large section of undeveloped land running directly across the heart of the New Berlin. Thus property development lobbies are added to those of archaeologists, politicians, survivors of the war and citizens of the new republic in the debate over how to 'develop' this area.

The site is currently sealed and political opinion remains divided on its future. A strong historical lobby maintains the value of the site is severely limited; indeed, the celebrated German historian, Professor Rürup, has intimated that the remains are of no historical interest and should simply be demolished. Such views are reiterated by Rainer Klemke (spokesman for the government's cultural senator) who has referred to the archaeologists' lobbying for preservation as 'moles who always want to preserve everything they come across. What is the point of keeping these things when it is all documented?' (Klemke, quoted in MacWilliam, 1995, p. 5). Yet to retain only the positive aspects of one's past and to obliterate all trace of the evil is to present a cultural and historical landscape that is, to say the least, incomplete.

Such debates have a clear historical echo in the arguments surrounding the development of the *Gestapo Gelände*. Since the Second World War much of the site had been either demolished or buried under war rubble and waste. In 1982 the Berlin Senate decided to reshape the landscape of the former Prinz-Albrecht-Polai (Rürup, 1989). Here, then, is a truly dark site providing a real dilemma for policy-makers and city government. This complex of former government buildings, museums, and a hotel in Niederkirchenstrasse and Prinz-Albrecht-Strasse had been the base of the SS, Gestapo and Reich Security forces. Here Himmler and the other Nazi leaders debated the Final Solution, the repression of internal resistance and organized and managed the state secret police. Among the remains were the ruins of the Gestapo torture cells buried under war rubble by a government more concerned with post-war reconstruction than modern German history.

Yet no consensus on development of a suitable memorial was reached and to catalyse some form of remembrance an organization calling itself the 'Active Museum of Fascism and Resistance in Berlin' issued an appeal to encourage volunteers to symbolically excavate Germany's buried past on 8 May 1985. In the event the 'excavators' found actual ruins of historical significance that came to be exhibited some two years later in the 'temporary' exhibit, 'The Topography of Terrors'. This exhibit remains the main orientation to this site and provides historical documentation of the prison cells, torture blocks and administrative buildings of the Nazi state organization. Admission is free and emphasis is on historical fact and authenticity.

The museum is sponsored by the Berlin Senate, administered by the Berliner Festspiele, and was officially opened to the public in 1988. It constitutes the covered excavation of the remains of the Gestapo headquarters building. The debris of the Allied bombing raid has become the exhibition. Reconstruction might be construed as an allusion to former glories so with both political and curatorial support the site has been left as a ruin. Such a display strategy is conscious and deliberate:

> To leave it in the form of debris, which does not allude to the structure that existed above except through historical legend and sober, distancing documentation, seemed an honourable solution. The historical display fragments the original narrative and replaces the original animating forces with distant representations. (Rürup, 1995, p. 136)

No attempts have been made to experiment with state-of-the-art interpretation techniques, rather, the focus is on the stark black-and-white records and photographs which provide the historical legacy for the building (for further coverage see Rürup, 1989).

The 'temporary' nature of the interpretation and the building in which it is housed was the result of a compromise for authorities who agonized over architectural competitions and political debates on what to do with this infamous site. Despite a range of innovative proposals it seems likely the ruins will remain untouched and the temporary exhibit will become the permanent mode of display. Interestingly, neither the building nor the exhibit has become a focus for neo-Nazi interest. No plans have been made for further development but this area provides an appreciation of how Germany has to continually struggle with its past to define its current reality.

Plötzensee Prison: an uneasy compromise

Berlin is also the location of the Plötzensee memorial. This memorial site well illustrates the ambiguities associated with commemoration and the ambiguities of sacrifice, genocide and resistance in the new Germany. The site known as Gedenkstätte Plötzensee is located in an industrial suburb of Berlin. It is Berlin's first memorial 'To the victims of the Hitler Dictatorship'. During the period of Nazi rule this was the site where numerous resistance fighters were hanged or guillotined. In 1952 the Berlin Senate enacted legislation to incorporate an urn with concentration camp soil to be located near the former prison in the courtyard entrance to both commemorate the resistance fighters who died in Plötzensee and in concentration camps throughout occupied Europe (Young, 1993).

In the execution room itself the stark interior is both sombre and chilling. Four hooks on which executioners hung their victims are installed. The infamous guillotine that existed here is not on display and interpretation is documentary, low key and clearly concerned with practical accounts of the dreadful use of this building.

3   *Plötzensee Memorial, Berlin*

However, this is also the site of the memorial to the Wehrmacht officers executed for their part in the failed plot to kill Hitler in 1944. Herein lies a dilemma at the heart of the memorial. The combination of a commemorative memorial to the plotters, many of whom were serving Nazi officers, and the victims of that regime is problematic. German resistance is invariably commemorated because it at least allows an accommodation of the horrors of the past. Yet here at Plötzensee political resistance and Jewish resistance victims are combined with a memorial to their former oppressors – an accommodation that relatives and former victims find difficult to accept (Young, 1993). Here a selective memory is being employed (to provide a positive memorial to national resistance) and self-idealization (combining both a conception of 'heroes' and victims). The Berlin Senate has appreciated the sacrifice of the resistance and recognized the extermination of the Jews in a joint commemoration to officers of the 1944 revolt. Such a process of linkage and nationalization of heritage creates discord but is an increasingly common occurrence in 'dark' sites of the Second World War.

The House of the Wannsee Conference

Located in the affluent suburbs of north Berlin on the shores of the Wannsee lake is the house in which those responsible for the planning of the 'final solution' to the Jewish 'problem' in Europe prepared their meticulous plans and schedules for the systematic execution of the Jewish race at the infamous Wannsee Conference. A German historian, Joseph Wulf originally drew attention to the historic significance of the site and proposed in 1965 the establishment of an 'International Documentation Centre for Recording National Socialism and its Consequences'. This plan was supported by the World Jewish Congress who, along with the Berlin Senate, aided development costs. It was established as a Holocaust Memorial site in 1986 and opened in 1992 on the 50th anniversary of the original Wannsee Conference in 1942. The site now combines a permanent exhibit, an educational department with out-reach facilities for schools and adult education, a multi-media library and a memorial and study centre. Visitor numbers total in excess of 170,000 per year and entrance is free. The permanent exhibition is

4   *House of the Wannsee Conference, Berlin*

housed in some thirteen chambers of the house and the clear emphasis in interpretation is 'History as a Learning Site' (House of the Wannsee Conference, 1992b). The exhibition attempts to unravel the extent to which the National Socialist politics of genocide were rooted in German tradition and aspects of everyday life for Germans over the period of 1939–45. As visitor information indicates clearly, the exhibition at this site 'addresses systematic preparation and planning, technical-bureaucratic perfection and inexorably accomplished mass murder as an administrative process carried out by the entire state apparatus and a host of accomplices who in part demonstrated their obedience with pre-emptive zeal' (House of the Wannsee Conference, 1992b).

The educative role of this facility is clearly apparent and includes out-reach facilities for discussion groups and seminars to be carried out by site 'scholars' outwith the facility in places of employment or educational institutions. Such facilities incorporate an active approach to interpretation of the period. Adopting the ideological position that only with open discussion and analysis will the full extent of involvement become apparent, as the information guide notes:

Almost every occupational group, every institution had some part in the discrimination and exclusion of the Jews, who were written off as undesirable encumbrances ('Ballastexistenzen'). Thus we must examine how and why the bureaucratic infrastructure in municipal and state administrations functioned with so little friction.

The novelty of our approach is to attempt to show students and working people – e.g. in nursing, police departments, rail transportation services and public administration – by way of relevant documents and trade journals from the Nazi era how their own occupational group was involved back then in carrying out the 'Final Solution'. (House of the Wannsee Conference, 1992b)

The actual interpretation is based on photography with detailed accompanying notes. Extensive quotations from documents and official state literature are used in what is a tangible attempt to bring to life the history and tragedy of this era.

Concentration camps in Germany

It must be remembered at the outset that major extermination was never planned to take place in Germany. Concentration camps here were the sites of death and torture but not on the scale of the camps in Poland. Indeed, as Young notes:

Had it not been for the massive, last ditch evacuations of Jewish prisoners from death camps in Poland, who died by the tens of thousands at the end of their forced marches back into Germany, the mass murder might have remained a foreign phenomena altogether. (Young, 1993, p. 53)

As a consequence, the interpretation of concentration camps in Germany is important not only as sites of atrocity but also in terms of how historians have approached the period from an historical/documentary perspective and how the victims of Fascism are commemorated. The most important German camp in terms of visitor numbers is Dachau, near Munich. With in excess of 900,000 visitors per year, it has already received considerable review by scholars in this field.

James Young, in his excellent treatment of this camp's history and critique of its memorial function, describes it as an icon for Western tourists. Dachau was not one of the major extermination camps yet ironically it remains one of the most visited. This stems largely from the influence of the media, its geographical proximity and its place in the collective memory of the camps' functions. Dachau featured heavily in the media presentation of its liberation and reportage of its on-site trials of camp guards and Nazi functionaries. It offers an excellent museum with carefully maintained grounds. However, it is almost a sanitized monument, well groomed and reinvented after many of the original buildings were lost following successive reuse in the period post-1945. Thus Dachau cannot provide an 'authentic' experience but rather an interpretative memorial experience. The primacy of many of the camp features has been lost in its reinvention.

Interestingly in the late 1950s and early 1960s the camp was overgrown and the nearby townspeople could no longer see its fences and towers and the Munich suburb/small town of Dachau began to re-establish itself 'free' of its 'dark' legacy. Indeed, when the renovation and development of the camp began and the camp's structure became clearly visible, the level of local resistance was considerable. It was part of a past that many wanted to leave behind yet, for the victims, their relatives and others, understanding required interpretation and rediscovery. As Baudrillard (1988, p. 23) noted: 'Forgetting the extermination is part of the extermination itself.' Thus Dachau became an icon because of its location, media image and redevelopment role in the media, but it is Sachsenhausen, north of Berlin, in the former GDR, that perhaps illustrates many of the new challenges such dark attractions now face.

Sachsenhausen: conflicting ideology and relativeness

Holocaust memorials in the former East Germany tend to be highly oriented towards all victims of Fascism and rarely detail the extent of Jewish loss. In many cases the dynamic of rebuilding under Communism

5   *Sachsenhausen KZ, Berlin*

has left little but place names on maps as a form of stylized remembrance (Young, 1993).

Following the fall of the Berlin Wall and the formation of a unified Germany the new administrators now have to deal with the ideological legacy of selective interpretation of the Communist era. As Radford has noted:

> After the Second World War, museums in former Nazi concentration camps in East Germany became little more than instruments of Communist propaganda. As shrines, where members of the Communist hierarchy portrayed themselves as heirs of the anti-Fascist struggle, these museums disregarded the fate of the Jews in the Holocaust or anomalies such as the 1936 pact between Hitler and Stalin. (1995, p. 29)

Sachsenhausen concentration camp, which is located in a residential suburb (Oranienburg) some 20 km north of Berlin, is a contemporary example of conflicting ideological interpretation of the extermination process and the post-war use of such camps. Although not an extermination camp *per se*, more than 100,000 prisoners are said to have lost their lives here and the burden of interpretation of this camp's dark history has now fallen to the administration of this economically depressed area of the new Germany.

The camp was built in a unique triangular shape designed and built by slave labour under the supervision of the Schutzstaffel (SS). Following the Second World War the East German authorities demolished many of the buildings within the original triangular boundary but outside a number of original SS buildings remain. It was only in 1961 that the government of the GDR agreed to open a memorial centre and exhibition. Yet the approach was clearly ideological and the interpretation selective. The exhibition's main focus was on the key role of the Soviet liberators and the fate of Communist prisoners. The plight of Social Democrats, homosexuals, Jews, Slavs, Jehovah's Witnesses and pacifists was simply not referred to. Some years later, following external pressure, an exhibit on Jewish-Communist detainees was also included: however, the gaps in the interpretation were far from bridged. Following the end of the Second World War the camp was used for the internment of a range of people deemed 'anti-social' or 'opponents' of the Communist regime in the period 1945–50.

In 1989 a number of mass graves from this period were uncovered outside the triangular boundary and a new focus in interpretation became necessary. Now both the Nazi *and* Soviet-dominated periods merit consideration. However, attempts to date to jointly commemorate the Nazi and Stalinist crimes have created tensions. The need to record, interpret and commemorate the victims of 1945–50 is part of a separate period of history which is distinct from the Nazi period and which merits full historical consideration and historical coverage (Bordage, 1993). Opinion of how this should be dealt with is divided at city administration levels and more locally by the curators at the site. The selective interpretation of the GDR can catalyse and produce a reactive display of the Soviet camp. Critics have challenged the conception of the Soviet internment as a continuation of the Nazi terror.

A further complication is that little is known about the operation of the camp except from eyewitness reports and detailed historical records are almost non-existent (Radford, 1995). Currently, the guide to the camp features the Nazi concentration camp and the Soviet Occupation

6   *Dissecting table, Sachsenhausen KZ, Berlin*

internment camp as distinct sections. Yet within what is now entitled the Sachsenhausen Memorial Centre there exists a second exhibition unrelated to the history of the camp either before or after 1945. It is entitled 'An Encyclopaedia of European Enmity against Jews'. It skilfully intersperses photographs, lithographs and historical records with historical coverage of the Jewish race from medieval times. It also incorporates an exhibition on Jewish life in Berlin in the early 1930s. By comparison, the use of the camp as a Soviet internment centre remains undeveloped.

The city authorities do not wholly share the perception of the camp as an important site of historical interpretation. Following an arson attack on the Jewish barracks 38 and 39 in 1992 a competition for the redesign of a large element of the camp was undertaken. The lower half of the Sachsenhausen 'triangle' was the subject of the architectural competition. Its aim was to stimulate redevelopment of the site that hopefully would have economic development benefits for the whole area of Dranenburg. The award-winning proposal for what the city viewed as sorely needed development was a plan for housing, incorporating the building of a health and beauty facility on the site of the former SS barracks. A second less controversial proposal by a Jewish architect (David Libeskind) proposed a combination of archaeological interpretation, memorial and the development of workshops, art studios, a museum, a computer training facility and horticultural development. Such developments are still being debated although the importance of investment and job creation is still seen as central to the development by local government.

The camp has also been plagued by local neo-Nazis who as recently as 1992 burnt down barracks 38 and 39, containing the Jewish prisoner exhibitions. Interestingly, this arson attack is to feature in the planned redevelopment of the huts in which the history of Jews in the camp and details of everyday camp life will be covered. Such recent events provide a new resonance to the task of interpretation in Sachsenhausen. Furthermore, the threat from neo-Nazis remains so serious that currently one-sixth of the camp's state and federal budget is devoted to security.

In spite of the ambivalent attitude of the city and the need for further documentation and renovation of the camp, it continues to attract

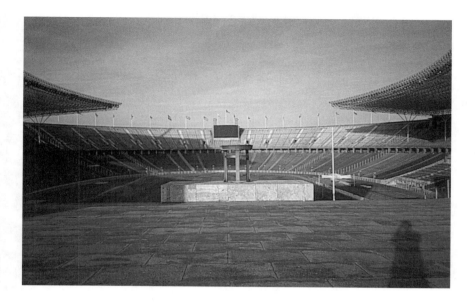

7   *Olympia Stadium, Berlin*

growing numbers of visitors. In excess of 250,000 were recorded in 1995, with over 100,000 from overseas. This site sits at the heart of debate over redevelopment. The development echoes some aspects of the arguments over the interpretation of the *Gestapo Gelände* and the controversial proposal to develop a supermarket on the site of Ravensbrück. Here another element of the dark periods of Germany's history creates a tension of development and relativism born out of disparate requirements in an emergent economy. The harsh realities of rebuilding industry, creating employment and stimulating growth present a strong counterpoint to that lobby who stress the centrality of an ideologically free interpretation of a history many would prefer to leave behind.

The Olympia Stadium, designed by Albert Speer, represents one of the few Nazi structures still used for its original purpose. Its brooding presence in Germany's new capital offers an immediate link to the 'other place' and to the dark past it represents.

CHAPTER FOUR

The Death Camps
of Poland

Poland was the centre of the Holocaust; throughout Poland the legacy and historical scars of Nazi occupation are found in the camps and museums of Majdanek, Lamsdorf, Zagan, Stutthof, Gross-Rosen, Radogoszcz, Treblinka and the tragic sights of commemoration; the Fort VII, Pozan: the Warsaw Citadel; Powiak Prison, Warsaw; the Zamosk Rotunda and the Gestapo museum in Warsaw (see Map 1.0).

The complex of Auschwitz–Birkenau represents perhaps one of the greatest dilemmas for interpretation. Here some 1.6 million people (90 per cent of them Jewish) were killed. During operation, the Auschwitz KZ consisted of three major parts and more than 40 sub-camps. The first part was Auschwitz (the main/mother camp known as *Stammlager*). It was established in Oswieczim in 1940 in an isolated location in former military barracks. The second part of the complex was Birkenau (sometimes known as Auschwitz II). It was built in 1941 some three miles from Oswieczim in a village called Brzezinka. Its original inhabitants were resettled to make way for the largest development of the entire Nazi system of concentration camps. It was in Birkenau that the main installations for mass killing (gas chambers and crematoria) were built (Swiebocka, 1995) (see Map 2.0 for location).

The third part of the camp was built on land adjacent to the IG Farben factory producing synthetic rubber and fuel, originally called Buna (later Monowitz). In addition, more than 40 sub-camps were located in nearby Silesia for accommodation and exploitation of slave labour (see Map 2.0). In this extermination centre, known as Birkenau

Map 1.0   Deportation railways to Auschwitz

(built on the site of a demolished village), the Germans killed some 1.6 million people (Young, 1993).

The camp was abandoned in 1944 by the Germans who set part of it on fire and dynamited crematoria and gas chambers. The liberating Red Army burned down several of the barracks at Birkenau while others were lost following the war as local residents used them for building materials. By 1947 the Polish parliament had declared the

8   *Auschwitz KZ, Oswieczim, Poland*

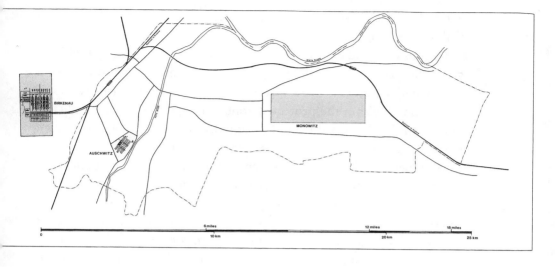

*Map 2.0   Map of Auschwitz, Birkenau and Monowitz
         (total installation 18 sq. miles)*

remainder of the camp would be preserved as a memorial to 'the martyrdom of the Polish nation and other peoples'. True international accord was not reached until 1977. Following later agreement, the work of the International Auschwitz Committee (IAC) achieved the designation of Auschwitz–Birkenau as a UNESCO World Cultural Heritage Site in 1973 (Goldstein, 1995).

Disputes over the extent of the camp and how much of it should be preserved remain unresolved. Originally, in 1947, the state museum of Oswieczim-Brzezinka occupied some 200 hectares (Chicago, 1993). This represented a compromise satisfying the essential elements of memorial with the need for reconstruction and redevelopment following the end of the Second World War. Fundamentally, Poles began to rebuild their lives in the ashes of the concentration camp. Residential and commercial development in the 1950s caused policy-makers to reconsider camp boundaries and in 1962 a protected zone was created in Brzezinka and any construction around the museum was to be abandoned. In 1977 the Polish Minister of Administration, Local Development and Environment extended the existing museum boundary further, to a distance of 500 metres from the perimeter of the museum. Indeed, by 1979, it was entered under these revised boundaries onto the UNESCO World Cultural Heritage List.

The museum and the ruins of the camp were surrounded by buildings which had risen chaotically in the post-war years in the absence of a clearly defined and extensive protective zone. In later years owners of land located within the protected zone felt deprived of their rights to build and develop on this land (originally confiscated by the Nazis). Further arguments arose over administrative inconsistency in respect of developments within the area which had occurred under Communism. Land claims continue to this day with occasional legal challenges to legitimacy of ownership occurring.

Following the fall of the Communist government, a re-approval of the boundary was debated and now a compromise position has been reached. Development is now permitted within the 500-metre zone but it must not conflict with the character of the museum and the memorial. The site of the museum is encompassed by an economically active hinterland and productive farm land and, following consultation with international bodies and local and national government, it was determined that in a situation such as this a compromise was required. In a site where the museum has become surrounded by buildings, 90 per cent of which were built after 1945, historical authenticity will be permanently illusive. It was deemed more effective to preserve the specific sites connected with the history of the camp and relax the artificial blockade against investment in the whole protected zone surrounding the site (Young, 1993). In this sense, life meets death and the new industry of Poland meets the darker industry that was the historical finality of Auschwitz–Birkenau. In such a case the site is distorted, being neither complete nor fully authentic. The distortion process, though recorded, is not always apparent in the reinstatement and refurbishment of buildings. The case is more confusing when such buildings are not central elements to the preservation of the site.

The authenticity of the camp, whether real or created, is apparent in its very landscape. Auschwitz III, the labour camp, supplying workers for the enormous IG Farben works has disappeared and is not part of any tourist itinerary. Similarly, the satellite camps of Brzeszce, Rajsko and Trzebinia are not visited and although the sites may be marked with state cenotaphs, no interpretation links them to Auschwitz. The 'reality' for the tourist is Auschwitz I, yet this is not the camp liberated by the Soviets in 1945 (Dwork and Van Pelt, 1994). The misrepresentation of history begins in the entrance to the car park of Auschwitz I. The visitor appears to be approaching the main entrance (an apparently more recent orientation point, built post-1945) but in fact they are already well within the boundaries of the 1945 camp. External to these tourist boundaries the buildings of the *Schutzhaftlagererweiterung* (extension of the protective custody camp) can be seen and they remain off limits to tourists. They appear both outside and distinct from the camp. These spacious structures are now used to accommodate the Polish army and to house low-income residents: their solid design and quality-build are in marked contrast to the barrack huts which are part of the collective memory of Auschwitz buildings. Yet these are as elemental a part of the camp as the other more memorable aspects.

Similarly, the multi-use entry building (designated by the architect of the Central Architectural Office as building KL/BW 160) which incorporates a post office, restaurant, cafeteria, currency exchange, cinema, retail outlet, hotel and conference room, was an important part of the former camp. Its appearance and quality of build look post-war

9 *Gates of Auschwitz II, Birkenau KZ, Oswieczim, Poland*

but it was in fact the prisoners' reception centre (Dwork and Van Pelt, 1994). Here the baptism into concentration camp life occurred in an architecture designed to take the captive from *Mensch* to *Untermensch*. Here prisoners were systematically registered, tattooed, surrendered their valuables, undressed, shaved, showered, and were left to dress in the regulation striped uniform of incarceration. The prisoners then left and entered the camp through the porch facing the 'Arbeit Macht Frei' gate. Yet the building remains unmarked and the tourist is left with only a partial understanding of the camp and its operation.

Commemoration

The conception of Auschwitz from the start was as a Polish/ Internationalist commemorative site. The barrack-houses were developed as national memorials of different countries' victims (see illustration from Guide book, Map 3.0). Thus a composite interpretation was offered of something that was clearly a predominantly Jewish tragedy (Young, 1993). This method of interpreting the Holocaust as a Polish tragedy was part of an overly political approach to history and distortion of heritage under the former Communist authorities.

Similarly, the famously incorrect inscription in twenty different languages on the black sarcophagus at the end of the railway line in Birkenau noted that 'Four million people suffered and died here at the hands of the Nazi murderers between the years 1940 and 1945' (quoted in Young, 1993). This type of interpretation contributes to what has been entitled heritage dissonance (Ashworth, 1996). The ideologically imbalanced treatment of the camp, coupled with the reputation for anti-Semitism that Poland had, contributed to a feeling of disinheritance and distance among Jews. Interpretation provided the reinforcement for the dominant Communist regime. The post-war government tried to portray themselves as heirs to all that was 'noble and victorious'. In such an interpretation there was little room for consideration of Nazi racist ideology and camps became monuments primarily to the victims of Fascism.

Following the end of the Communist regime such an interpretation was simply removed and the more accurate count of 1.6 million has been

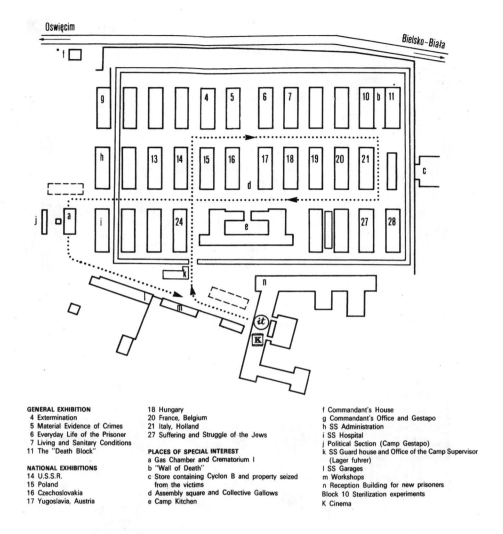

Map 3.0   Plan of the former concentration camp KL Auschwitz I

generally accepted. The inflation of the figure came about partially as a result of the Soviet authorities wishes to promote the loss of socialist lives in the international fight against Fascism, and partially as a result of the Polish authorities exaggerating the extent of their own losses. With the fall of the Communist government, a commission was convened to consider the future of the museum. Jewish Holocaust scholars were asked

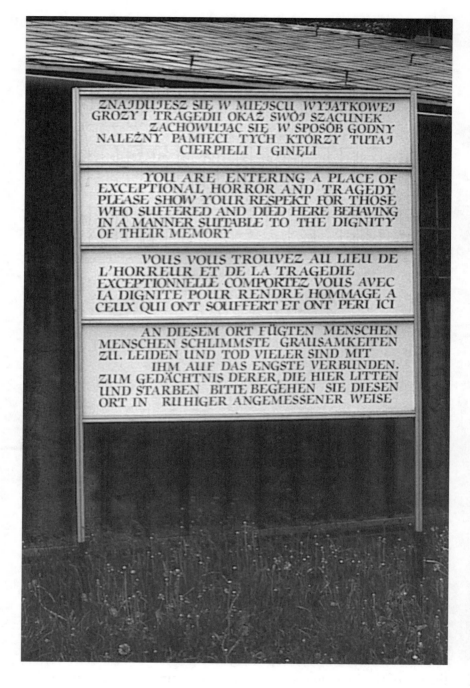

10   *Sign from Lidice, Czech Republic*

for guidance and a move towards redressing the imbalance of interpretation was set in motion. Thus was appointed the International Auschwitz Council, whose task has been to redress the Marxist bias and manipulation of this site.

Specifically, the committee recommended that Auschwitz–Birkenau museum show clearly that:

1. this was the site where 1.6 million men, women, and children were murdered;
2. 90-plus per cent of those were Jews;
3. large numbers of non-Jews (especially Poles) died at Auschwitz;
4. both Jews and non-Jews murdered there were from all walks of life, a range of political persuasions, a variety of cultural, religious, and national traditions;
5. the atrocities committed at Auschwitz were perpetrated by the German National Socialist regime and its collaborators. (Young, 1993)

In addition to the above general agreement on the main tenets of interpretation, it was accepted that in the redevelopment and reorientation of the museum a large consultation process with the full range of Holocaust research organizations and survivors groups should be undertaken. Practical aspects of reorientation included setting up a shuttle bus between Auschwitz I and Birkenau, providing an historical orientation for visitors upon entry, and reviewing inscriptions and signs. Recruitment and training of guides were standardized, and audio tours were to be provided to those without a guide. Furthermore, kosher food was to be permanently available in the museum restaurant.

Formats of interpretation

Entrance to the museum is free and guides are offered in various languages which are accessed via registering nationality on entry. These, plus the written guide, are the main written format of orientation. In Auschwitz I, visitor orientation commences with the cinema

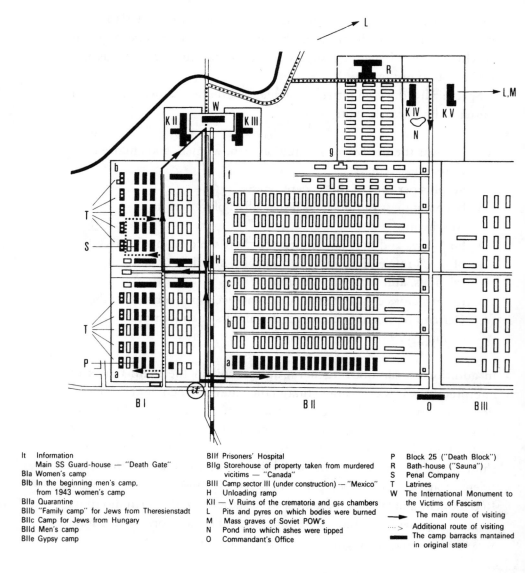

It	Information				
	Main SS Guard-house — "Death Gate"	BIIf	Prisoners' Hospital	P	Block 25 ("Death Block")
BIa	Women's camp	BIIg	Storehouse of property taken from murdered	R	Bath-house ("Sauna")
BIb	In the beginning men's camp,		vicitims — "Canada"	S	Penal Company
	from 1943 women's camp	BIII	Camp sector III (under construction) — "Mexico"	T	Latrines
BIIa	Quarantine	H	Unloading ramp	W	The International Monument to
BIIb	"Family camp" for Jews from Theresienstadt	KII — V	Ruins of the crematoria and gas chambers		the Victims of Fascism
BIIc	Camp for Jews from Hungary	L	Pits and pyres on which bodies were burned		The main route of visiting
BIId	Men's camp	M	Mass graves of Soviet POW's		Additional route of visiting
BIIe	Gypsy camp	N	Pond into which ashes were tipped		The camp barracks mantained
		O	Commandant's Office		in original state

11   Map of Auschwitz KZ, Auschwitz II-Birkenau Oswieczim, Poland

presentation which focuses on the liberation of the camp in 1945.
Scheduled showings in a range of languages are offered to provide
tourists with a starting-point. The footage was taken by Soviet troops
who liberated the camp in 1945. The bulk of the camp consists of the
prison cell blocks (see Map 3.0) which are devoted to national memorials

12   *Exhibit of Zyklon B gas canisters, Auschwitz KZ, Oswieczim, Poland*

of the dead of many nations. These huts do not offer a chronological or coherent orientation or guidance to the history of the camp. There are also a number of huts used for the possessions of murdered inmates; there are rooms full of clothes and suitcases, toothbrushes, dentures, glasses. Block II (see Map 3.0) is the location of the first experiments undertaken with Zyklon B gas on prisoners and nearby is the infamous Death Wall where thousands of prisoner executions took place.

The interpretation assumes a knowledge of the camps and their purpose. Explanation, orientation and historical documentation are limited. In the larger barracks entitled 'Jews', the displays are reverential as opposed to historical or sequential. In the floor above this there is a detailed display on the Jewish resistance, yet it is the location of the Jewish commemoration, simply within the other displays, that is disconcerting. Despite other recent attempts to redress the imbalance of interpretation (see, for example, Piper, 1992), this is an aspect of the camp that needs review. Birkenau, which is much less visited than Auschwitz, covers more than 425 acres and formerly comprised some 300-plus buildings. (See Map 4.0.) Approximately 60 buildings remain and the ruins of the others can be easily traced. The railway line, sidings and platforms remain, as do some of the huts with their pitifully bare wooden bunks. However, Birkenau remains considerably underdeveloped in comparison to Auschwitz I (see Figure 11). The official guided tour is limited in both time and geographical coverage and does not include a visit to the major crematoria, the real site of the genocide.

The assumption of prior knowledge is also evident in Birkenau, where the presentation of information has been operationalized via signage on black granite blocks serving as mini-monuments and making a clear analogy with the stones covering graves on which 'real' information and 'real' history are displayed. The aim of the interpretation is to stimulate reflection and contemplation rather than an historical/literal interpretation to catalyse an 'understanding and appreciation' of the past. Auschwitz I was designated a permanent exhibit in post-war Poland; a signpost location for the Poles in the commemoration of the Holocaust. Furthermore, one museum was realistically all that could be expected in a country undergoing massive post-war reconstruction. Indeed, the focus on Auschwitz I and the erosion of the historical reality of camp boundaries and geography are further emphasized in the scale model of the crematoria II (a Birkenau structure relocated in Auschwitz I) and the transportation of spectacles, hair, suitcases, etc., from Birkenau to Auschwitz. In this way the museum (of Auschwitz I) is given a new identity and 'blurs' the location of the actual site of mass execution (Dwork and Van Pelt, 1994).

Interpretation of such elemental sites of European history continually has to be managed with care. Its relationship to tourism and its potential appearance as spectacle and entertainment are problematic. This situation becomes acute particularly when offered to a tourist public who are invariably curious about suffering, horror and death. Horror and death have become established commodities, on sale to tourists who have an enduring appetite for the darkest elements of human history (Uzzel, 1989).

International involvement in the interpretation and operation of the camp has helped the Polish authorities who in the climate of the post-Communist reconstruction have reduced the maintenance budget radically. Indeed, money for new displays or major restoration projects is increasingly sought externally. For example, the former US Ambassador to Austria, Donald Lauder, has developed a personal foundation to raise

13 *Site of crematoria, Auschwitz KZ, Oswieczim, Poland*

more than $40 million for the purposes of long-term maintenance and presentation of the camp. In recent years it is the large exhibit of human hair on display in Block Four in Auschwitz I that has catalysed debate. The hair on display (almost two tons in total) has begun to decay. The previous Polish preservation methods were ineffectual. This hair, originally used by German industry for the war effort, is now troubled by insect infestation and rot, and the preservation of such a large exhibit is a unique task for curators and conservationists. Some insist that its preservation is vital whereas others are less convinced of the requirement for such remains to be displayed. Young argues that:

> These artefacts also force us to recall the victims as the Germans have remembered them to us: in the collected debris of a destroyed civilization. For, by themselves, these remnants rise in a macabre dance of memorial ghosts. Armless sleeves, eyeless lenses, headless caps, footless shoes: victims are known only by their absence, by the moment of their destruction. In great loose piles, these remnants remind us not of the lives that once animated them, so much as of the brokenness of lives. For when the memory of a people and its

past are reduced to the bits and rags of their belongings, memory of life itself is lost. What of the relationships and families sundered? What of the scholarship and education? The community and its traditions? Nowhere among this debris do we find traces of what bound people together into a civilization, a nation, a culture. Heaps of scattered artefacts belie the interconnectedness of lives that made these victims a people. The sum of these dismembered fragments can never approach the whole of what was lost. That a murdered people remains known in Holocaust museums anywhere by their scattered belongings, and not by their spiritual works, that their lives should be recalled primarily through the images of their death, may be the ultimate travesty. (1993, pp. 132–3)

However, the very notoriety and worldwide knowledge of some of these exhibits – the hair, shoes, the spectacles – can reduce the emotive reaction and harden the visitors. In this way, the emotion is lost, reduced by knowledge in anticipation and familiarity from media images (Lanzmann, 1995a).

Tourist behaviour at the site has also prompted intense debate among the International Auschwitz Committee (IAC). The idea of a behaviour and dress-code was, however, discarded. As Young noted in his coverage of this debate:

'No way', shot back an incredulous American. 'How are we going to force stuffy Western modes of dress on seven hundred thousand tourists a year, from all over the world? How are these tourists supposed to dress?' The American acknowledged that a dress code might pose no hardship on British visitors, or even on the Poles, who often travel in their Sunday best anyway. But by forbidding shorts and sandals, for example, the committee might automatically exclude half the Israelis who travel here. As a compromise, it was agreed that an ambiguous invitation to decorum might be posted instead, just to remind visitors that this memorial is, if not a holy site, also not just another tourist haven. (1993, p. 153)

During the author's period of fieldwork at Auschwitz–Birkenau the extent of commodification of the process of visiting the camp became

14   *Hair/shoes exhibit from Auschwitz KZ, Oswieczim, Poland*

clear. Groups of schoolchildren were taking photographs of each other, parents were photographing their children at the gates of Birkenau and, indeed, school parties were sitting on the ruins of the crematorium eating sandwiches. One is also aware that tourists follow a relatively short itinerary of approximately 90 minutes if they are here as part of an organized party. Clearly, to cover the full nature of either Auschwitz or Birkenau would take considerably longer.

Significant debates centred upon the conservation of the camp which presents a huge dilemma for curators. The decay of the camp, its barbed wire, barrack-houses and ruins is a continual process of erosion. The size of the area means that there is a constant need to record and monitor the condition of buildings (never intended as permanent construction works by their Nazi architects). Furthermore, the growth of vegetation and foliage-coverage has to be managed and controlled. The barbed wire has been the subject of replacement, simply because original wires have decayed.

In this case the place of death is itself dying. The camp, which was never built to last, has begun to decay on a massive scale. This should not be unexpected, as much of the camp was of course built by slave labour, with low grade materials and without proper foundations. As Ascherson has noted:

> The wire fences, stretching away in perspective to the misty horizon, are rusty and beginning to show gaps. The posts still carry their white insulators, but they are discoloured and starting to fragment. The surviving huts at Birkenau (most of them were burnt down after liberation, because they were crawling with typhus-infected lice) are rotting away. The steel rails which brought the cattle-wagons of doomed Jews up to the Birkenau ramp are still hard and clear, but the stones of the track-bed are vanishing beneath earth and weeds. (1995, pp. 12–13)

The process of repair necessary to counteract decay is not always clear to the tourist. The renewal of a number of the huts in Birkenau and the restoration of the first gas chamber at Auschwitz I are not made apparent to visitors and the authenticity of exhibits has been the cause of debate. Not clearly marked as a facsimile, it can be as deceptive as the guide who recalled to the authors: 'At Birkenau it is not exhibitionary. All is real' (Birkenau guide in conversation with authors, Birkenau, 1995). Yet Birkenau is a location which has endured significant change: the main extermination centre suffered substantial loss after the war. The unburned barracks were often destroyed for firewood or used in the construction of new homes for displaced Poles following the Second World War. The reconstruction of the crematoria in Auschwitz I was part of the museum development. The IAC felt a recreated crematoria was necessary as a culmination to the Auschwitz I tour. Consequently a chimney, gas chamber and two to three furnaces have been re-created. Reality is the crematoria and gas chambers of Birkenau some three to four miles away yet this is rarely the tourists' experience.

The authenticity of many aspects of the camp can rightly be questioned: the reinstated barracks, the barbed wire, the guard towers and the railway tracks which have been re-laid on new foundations since 1945 are all problematic. The historical primacy of many of the objects has been displaced. Yet to simply recreate the camp as new has been the subject of severe criticism. As Ceserani of the Wiener Library, London, has argued:

> There should be management rather than restoration. Decay has to be arrested, but the decay has become part of the character of the camp. It should be freeze-dried. To clean it up is disastrous. This is a terrible, terrible mistake. (Ceserani, quoted in Caseby and Goldman, 1994, p. 7.4)

Beyond the 'boundary' of the camp the reality of commercial activity once again intrudes. In the immediate vicinity (just outside of the main entrance to Auschwitz I), a range of private retail units have developed. Everything from hot dog stands, booksellers, postcard vendors, film stores and discount pottery warehouses are to be found. This, and the internal sale of concentration camp memorabilia, present the camp authorities with a clear dilemma. This dark attraction has swelled visitor numbers and catalysed economic activity.

Auschwitz after Communism

Following the fall of the Communist government, reorganization led to a museum covering approximately 200 hectares, incorporating over 150 buildings, and the ruins of more than 300. The museum also includes the prisoners' barracks, guard towers, railway sidings, side tracks, platforms and many kilometres of camp fencing. Just after 1990 over 200 people are employed in the museum in a range of activities including: conservation of buildings and relics; documentation; the collection of art works relating to the camp; archive research and maintenance; education; publishing and administration (Swiebocka, 1995). Such a World Heritage site presents policy-makers and tourist officials with a dilemma. Indeed, the relationship between the city of Krakow and the nondescript industrial town of Oswieczim to the sprawling dark site that is Auschwitz remains problematic. The tourist brochure for the town of Oswieczim concentrates on the town's long history and resists either mentioning Auschwitz by name, illustrating it with a photograph, or professing directions. As the brochure text notes in circumspect fashion:

> World War II was the most tragic period in the history of the town because of the concentration camp founded here during the war. Now it is a National Museum. But Oswieczim is also a town with its present day, interesting past and above all, its future. (*Oswieczim Tourist Information Brochure*, 1995, p. 3)

Young (1993) notes similar attempts in the German town of Dachau (near Munich), wherein the Mayor through the local tourist office attempts to market the Bavarian town. The sign at the entrance to Dachau Concentration Camp invites the visitor to: 'Visit Dachau the 1200 year old artist's centre with its castle and surrounding park. Offering a splendid view over the country.' Over the sign someone had scrawled 'HAVE YOU NO SHAME' in English and German (Chicago, 1993, p. 38). The tourist authority remains left with a 'public relations' problem that is intractable.

Such selective representation of the history of this small town is to some extent echoed in Krakow, where the wider historical and cultural elements of the city, and its history, are promoted as opposed to the nearby site of extermination. Yet the popularization of Thomas Keneally's book *Schindler's Ark* by the production of Steven Spielberg's film *Schindler's List* caused tourism to increase significantly in the 1993–4 period. In effect, 'Schindler tourism' developed, focusing on the remaining cluster of synagogues, cemeteries, and strongest of all, the disused film sets for the Schindler production. The film sets located near to Krakow became a Schindler tour in the years 1994–5. They were nearer, more contained and less time-consuming to visit than travelling to and reviewing the real camps of Auschwitz I and Birkenau.

The development of Auschwitz–Birkenau is a major challenge and a central element in understanding the phenomena of dark tourism. Clearly, the technological input to the development of the US Holocaust Memorial Museum or the Museum of Tolerance in Los Angeles as dynamic, educative and challenging facilities has relevance to how this site might develop. Yet a learning/orientation centre is necessary to prepare visitors for the camp and to acquaint them with the political and historical preconditions that made the Holocaust possible. In its current state the camp remains mute, its message partly distorted and poorly told.

CHAPTER FIVE

Covering History: The Interpretation of the Channel Islands Occupation, 1939–45

Governments have been pivotal in many aspects of interpretation and development of sensitive sites. From the demolition of the Cromwell Street residence of the murderers Fred and Rosemary West to the debates that raged long and hard over the development of the Sixth Floor in Dallas, Texas, herein lies an ideological dilemma for policy-makers ostensibly concerned with the issues of documentation, interpretation of reality and maintaining their educative mission. The Channel Islands during the period of German occupation offer just such a dilemma. Certain aspects of the occupation are acceptable to interpret and other dark elements are ignored. This is indicative of a selective memory of an event that is reinforced through interpretation.

The occupation of British soil during the Second World War is an emotive issue and the Channel Islands in that period have been the subject of a number of studies and historical reviews (see, for example, Toms, 1967; Cruickshank, 1975; King, 1991; and, more recently, Bunting, 1995). The legacy of the occupation in the form of concrete fortifications, museums, and the German Underground Hospital Museum on Jersey are now major tourism sites. Indeed, Jersey Tourism (the island tourist organisation) notes that:

The 'ill wind' of the war years has been turned to the good. The relics and remains of Hitler's British stronghold have now taken their place, both chronologically and commercially, alongside the older and more venerable attractions of the islands' heritage. The sightseeing circuit of war curiosities is now well established. Jersey's

German occupation is now big business, with more war museums per square mile than anywhere else in Europe. (1995a, p. 2)

Indeed, the 'Fortress Guernsey' campaign has made a feature of the defence structures of Guernsey, a neighbouring Channel Island. The advertising campaign 'Visit a Thousand Years of Fortifications' features extensive photographic representation of the island's defence from medieval times through to the Second World War. This has been particularly successful in encouraging holiday makers to combine tourism with wartime reminiscences. Yet, in the Channel Islands, residents lived under Nazi occupation and, as is the case of remembrance of traumatic events, a 'collective memory' has developed to deal with aspects of the period 1940–5 (Bunting, 1995). The same reappraisal of the past was noted in respect of the Kennedy assassination (1963) wherein the media had a central part in defining the reality of the traumatic event for the US people (Zelizer, 1992). In the case of the Channel Islands' occupation, Bunting has noted:

Here British communities lived under Nazi occupation, and their social fabric was stretched to breaking-point. Since the war, that fabric has been darned and patched, and its unity has been reconstructed by the development of a collective memory which erases divisions, and formulates a past most can accept. (1995, p. 4)

Interpretation of the occupation similarly commemorates, in the main, a view of the islands which is sanitized and avoids elements which might compromise the islanders' self-history. The aspects of occupation such as collaboration, fraternization and compromise are in most cases avoided. Yet here was a part of Britain occupied by the Nazis for five years and the location for forced labour and concentration camps operated by the feared Organisation Todt (OT). Yet, in tourism terms, these darker elements of history are both avoided and compromised. The Channel Islands Occupation and Liberation Temporary Exhibit at the Imperial War Museum similarly dealt with the more acceptable aspects of occupation – the realities of people's lives, the reduced diet – and only occasionally referring to the brutality, through the presence of a whip, and maps indicating where forced labour camps existed. But in truth, this made up little more than 5 per cent of total exhibition space. The issue of collaboration is dealt with interestingly. As one wall panel noted:

Some islanders collaborated with the Germans and in the islands, as in all countries under Nazi occupation, there was passive and active collaboration. Many people simply tried to get on with their lives and saw passive co-operation as the only way to maintain a safe and stable existence. A minority actively collaborated with the occupying forces. The most despised were those who informed against their neighbours, sometimes just to settle old scores . . . When the war ends, no one wants to admit to collaboration until hard evidence can be produced, so this uncomfortable subject has been literally ignored or forgotten except by those who suffered as a result of it. (Wall Panel, Imperial War Museum – Channel Islands Occupation and Liberation Temporary Exhibition)

This whole issue of collaboration is dealt with in only one museum on Jersey (the German Underground Hospital Museum) in a minor display area. Collaboration remains a highly sensitive issue, as the Public Relations Consultant for the German Underground Hospital Museum noted:

There was never collaboration in the manner in which it happened in France for instance. There was never an active movement here desperately seeking it in the way that there was in France. There was also never the trade with the Germans in the same way that there was in France. There were black marketeers here but they worked for themselves, they weren't actually working for the Germans in the way that they did in France. (Tabb, 1995, p. 20)

The defensive comparison made with France and the idea that a collaborationist works independently as some kind of wartime entrepreneur is, of course, revealing.

However, interestingly, the Imperial War Museum, which was the key agent in the development of this exhibition in partnership with the states of Guernsey and the states of Jersey occupation and liberation committees, does not feature in great detail the issue of the Jews, and the Jewish question was essentially ignored in this exhibition. Rather, the temporary exhibition at the Imperial War Museum focused on aspects of life under occupation, the level of resistance, the problems of resistance and the liberation in detail. Indeed, it is the liberation which has dominated the interpretation of occupation more than any other aspect, and represents how the collective memory focuses on the positive aspects.

The wholesale reluctance to interpret these sites stands in sharp contrast to the treatment of concentration camps elsewhere in Europe. While these were by no means death camps, dealing with the annihilation of large numbers of people, they left a scar on these islands that merits greater consideration. Similarly, the passivity with which the islanders responded contrasts with the vigorous resistance which developed in almost every other part of occupied Europe and, once again, questions the belief that Britain alone stood against Hitler and his forces during the difficult times of the Second World War.

Organisation Todt and the Channel Islands

The Third Reich employed islanders in the Organisation Todt (OT). This was the voluntary and forced slave labour organization that fuelled the German occupation forces. It was a Nazi organization that operated the infamous politics of race and classified its workforce along such lines. OT camps existed on Jersey, Guernsey and Alderney, as they did across all of occupied Europe. The role of the prisoners was to serve the occupation forces in defence-related war duties. As a consequence, their legacy is the concrete gun emplacements, the batteries, and the defence structures, in the construction of which many prisoners died. However, the commemoration of the existence of such forced labour camps is almost non-existent on the islands. Furthermore, the tales of abuse that were perpetrated on slave workers (on Alderney particularly) receive scant attention. The four OT camps on Alderney – Borkum, Helgoland, Norderney and Sylt – are now overgrown and not marked on tourist maps. There is a wholesale lack of interpretation and omission of these sites in guides (*Day Visitors' Guide to Alderney*, 1995). The perception of the events on Alderney and its relationship to the other islands was illustrated by the PR Consultant (and Jersey resident) for the German Underground Hospital Museum:

15   Gate and entrance, Borkum KZ, Alderney

> People over here and in Guernsey can effectively divorce themselves
> from it [the Alderney mass killings] completely because there was
> virtually nobody on Alderney so therefore what went on in Alderney
> was a nothing to do with us sort of thing. (Tabb, 1995, p. 25)

This selective perception of what is acceptable and pertinent is evidence
of the 'distance' that has developed with the collective memory. A focus
on liberation is clearly more palatable than a focus on the incarceration
and killings that occurred on Alderney. As the above commentator noted,
'it [mass killing on Alderney] is not relevant really to the experience of
the islands as a whole. You can't say what happened in Alderney was a
microcosm of what was happening because it wasn't' (Tabb, 1995, p. 26).

Similar omissions exist on Guernsey and, indeed, no public memorial
has ever been erected on either island (Guernsey and Alderney) in
commemoration of the deaths of slave labourers. In other parts of Europe
such sites have become centres of documentary interpretation (see, for
example, p. 111, for the documentary treatment of the SS headquarters
in Berlin, 'The Topography of Terrors'). Alternatively, some sites have
become gardens of remembrance and archive museums (for example,

16   *German Underground Hospital, Jersey*

Terezin (near Prague) in the Czech Republic). Yet on Alderney the sites of the notorious camps of Sylt and Norderney are unmarked and uninterpreted. This is made more disturbing since Alderney was the site of the UK's largest mass murder. The combination of conditions of cruelty, malnourishment and brutality produced a death toll between 1942 and 1945 that would be in thousands (Bunting, 1995). As Bunting notes in respect of such an omission: 'Only when there are exhibits in all the islands' museums to these people, and well-cared-for memorials and plaques in their memory . . . will they [the islanders] have begun to tell the whole story of the occupation' (1995, p. 336).

In contrast, the amount of coverage and investment in other aspects of the occupation and its interpretation for tourists is questionable. The single biggest tourist attraction after the Zoo on Jersey is the German Underground Hospital Museum, a labyrinth site which has been developed with detailed interpretation. The majority of its interpretation deals with the issues of operation and development of a hospital of this size, although its actual use was not great over the period of occupation. Similarly, a number of military museums and museums of occupation have been developed in bunker sites and emplacements throughout the islands (see,

17   *Liberation Memorial, St Helier, Jersey*

for example, St Peter's Bunker, St Peter's Village; Island Fortress Occupation Museum, St Helier; The Channel Islands Military Museum, St Oven). These, and the treatment of the occupation by the tourist organizations, tend to rely on documentary evidence of German occupation and a vision of island living conditions under occupation. Hardships such as lack of food and availability of shopping supplies are constantly referred to (see, for example, interpretation of the occupation at the Jersey Experience and the Jersey Museum, St Helier). Similarly, the investment and concentration on liberation and the production of liberation statues and tapestries in the centre of Jersey are indicative of how both the island government and the tourist authority wish to see the occupation remembered. Indeed, 1995 constituted the fiftieth anniversary of liberation and was the focus for celebration (Jersey Tourism, 1995b, p. 1). As Jersey Tourism (1995c) noted in a press release titled 'Our Dear Channel Islands', 'Jersey has celebrated freedom every year since the liberation with its own special bank holiday on 9 May'. Notably, the single largest commemoration of this period is the Liberation Sculpture 'specially commissioned to celebrate the liberation and 50 years of freedom . . . the focal point of Liberation Square, St Helier' (Jersey Tourism, 1995d). This point was reinforced in an interview with the Jersey Tourism PR Director who clearly indicated the focus of celebrations: 'What we wanted to do, and this is from a tourism aspect, was to talk about it in terms of celebrating liberation' (Needham, 1995, p. 6).

Clearly, the liberation and the celebrations of the end of the occupation have provided the focus for much of the interpretation. By contrast, it is the wholesale lack of interpretation of the darker elements that causes greater concern. This is not limited solely to Organization Todt and the issue of the concentration camps but is also, perhaps more sinisterly, avoided in the treatment of Jews on the island over this period.

The islanders and the Jewish question

As Bunting has noted: 'The Jewish issue is the most clear-cut example of where the island governments' co-operation with the Germans tipped into outright collaboration' (1995, p. 114). This is an incredibly sensitive aspect of the occupation, and while the islands' Jewish population was quite small, it is very apparent that their welfare was not considered important enough to jeopardize the working relationship enjoyed by the states government with the German occupation forces. It is a fact that three Jewish women were incarcerated, deported from the islands and sent to concentration camps, and it was apparent that many islanders acquiesced to such racist treatment and, by their own lack of intervention, were not directly involved in any form of resistance against this. It is perhaps the island governments' sensitivity in respect of not damaging these relationships with the occupation forces that led to this degree of compromise in the treatment of Jews on the islands.

Most of the Jewish population had left the islands in the evacuation carried out in anticipation of the occupation. Indeed, businesses belonging to Jews were auctioned off, and many islanders made a considerable fortune from taking over such businesses in the absence of the evacuated Jews. However, a number of Jewish residents did remain and anti-Jewish measures were introduced and reinforced in the laws of the state's government. This is interesting because clearly here German laws were introduced as part of Crown legislation on the islands. Thus, directly on British soil, the worst excesses of the Nazi regime in terms of racial and religious classification were being legitimized.

Clearly, then, British civil servants and members of the police had co-operated in sending a small minority of the British Jewish community to the gas chambers in the same way as other European governments had done. This is an aspect of the history of the occupation that receives very little coverage and the acquiescence of servants of the British government and British interest in the Channel Islands certainly merits greater analysis. What exists in the interpretation is a version of the occupation history that is a collective reappraisal of the more acceptable aspects of behaviour during the occupation. Focus is given to joyous events such as liberation and the entertaining aspects of occupation (fortifications, German memorabilia, etc.). What is not being dealt with here is the moral complexity of the situation, and indeed, the difficult questions of behaviour under occupation. As in all countries, the occupation compromised those who faced it on a daily basis and individuals were constantly presented with moral choices. In the islands it represents an uneasy accommodation which is most apparent in the treatment of the occupation in history books and the way in which the history of the islands is now re-interpreted as a tourist attraction. As we have seen elsewhere, the fascination with such darker aspects of history is considerable and, indeed, the islands have been able to capitalize on actively selling their wartime history (cf. Jersey Tourism, 1995b). However, it is the omissions that are important. What emerges is an island population who clearly did not rise up to fight the occupying forces but, rather, endured a period of occupation over a hard, dull five years which was generally peaceful. Over this period, approximately 50 per cent of the population were working in the employ of the Nazi German government. The extent of collaboration and fraternization will invariably be difficult to judge but what is also interesting is the lack of punishment of collaborators. Indeed, the wholesale absence of retribution following the occupation is intriguing. As Bunting notes in her valuable study of the area:

> No German was tried by the British on the islands, or in Germany, for wartime activities on the Channel Islands. No islanders were tried. No criticism was voiced of any of the island governments' actions during the occupation. Instead the bailiffs, Victor Carey and Alexander Coutanche, were knighted and other senior members of the occupation governments were also awarded honours. (1995, p. 277)

Yet in reports conducted by Theodore Pantcheff of MI19 following allegations of appalling atrocities committed on the island of Alderney among POWs, evidence emerges of crimes against humanity and clear responsibility among the Germans during the time of mass killings (1942–3). Pantcheff, along with Major Gruzdef from the London-based Soviet military mission, interviewed approximately 3,000 POWs to consider allegations of atrocity and it was quite apparent that there was substantial evidence of abuse. Yet following liberation there were no trials, a fact unusual in the extreme since following the liberation in countries like The Netherlands, prosecutions of war criminals went on for some years after 1945. Similarly, treatment of collaborators following the war was also non-judgemental and, indeed, there were no major investigations or trials for alleged collaboration following liberation in 1945.

The interpretation of the occupation of the Channel Islands throws into question the general interpretation of Britain's wartime stance. The idea of an island uninvaded and a people who stood against the Nazi foe, victorious in their resistance, is clearly compromised by the period of five years occupation (Bunting, 1995). More importantly, this occupation, and its subsequent interpretation in tourism sites, has a number of key omissions. Few of the tourist attractions make reference to slave labour, the treatment of the islands' Jewish population, fraternization and resistance that went on. Rather, as in the case of texts in the area (see, for example, Cruickshank, 1975; and Toms, 1967), they concentrate on military aspects, architecture and how the civilians dealt with the paucity of resources and living conditions. The selectivity of the interpretation in respect of the treatment of the forced labour camps (OT) is enlightening. In only a few instances are there real attempts to interpret what actually went on. Most important in this respect is the work of Joe Miere, the former curator of the Jersey German Underground Hospital Museum. Miere has put together a detailed exhibition on resistance and collaboration, detailing efforts of the islanders to resist the German occupation and going so far as to show and record photographs of famous collaborators. His honest desire was to recount both sides of the occupation story but this is an account which fits with difficulty into the German Underground Hospital Museum, a tourist attraction dealing with the more sensationalist aspects of wartime architecture. Clearly, such a radical interpretation challenges the approach adopted in other sites which reflect the defensiveness and insecurity in dealing with their own past. The real story of occupation upsets not only the British perception of an island nation standing heroically against a foe, but also upsets the islanders' own distorted celebration of the war. Historically, the Channel Islands represent a small aspect of the history of the Second World War. However, how British communities lived under Nazi occupation, and more importantly for this text, how the interpretation of those lives has been moulded and shaped to reflect a collective perception which offers us an uneasy accommodation of real events, is important. Islanders did fraternize and collaborated, working with the Germans (as did those in occupied countries throughout Western Europe), but it is only when such interpretation is comfortable with the reluctance of those living under occupation to champion the Jewish cause, to question the slave labour camps and to acknowledge the sacrifices made by the resistance, will historically acceptable interpretation be evident. Currently what exists is a selective perception and level of interpretation that is, at best, misguided and, at worst, deceptive.

CHAPTER SIX

The Death Site
of a President

One of the most infamous assassinations of the twentieth century was that of US President John F. Kennedy on 22 November 1963. How one interprets this event and the controversies surrounding it provide a contrasting approach to life/death interpretation in the USA.

Gravity and reverence are not always characteristic of death sites/ grave sites. Jim Morrison's grave in Père Lachaise in Paris questions the whole Victorian bourgeois cultural view of the cemetery as a place of dignity and mourning. Now tourists rather than mourners visit and undertake cemetery tours. This is a phenomenon that is well developed in the USA and in both Washington and Los Angeles there are good examples of the changing designation of such sites to convey tourism or leisure significance, both having developed organized cemetery tours by minibus. Indeed, JFK's own grave site has been seamlessly commodified into an 8-minute stop on a guided tour bus. Such treatments can be contrasted with the 'Death Park' located in the Phillipines, a respectful interpretation of graves and a celebration of the sites of typical graves and mausoleums. Clearly, this is a culturally specific example which sharply contrasts with other South East Asian treatments, namely, the infamous Precious Gold Mountain and Happy Peace Garden, Taiwan, which is much closer in operation to the commercial exploitation found in the USA and Western Europe (Palmer, 1993).

JFK: fascination and interpretation

The Kennedy phenomenon can be seen as both a media 'product' and a result of the availability of global news communication at the time of the assassination. The enduring fascination with the death of the former President posed authorities with the need to represent both his life and death. The form of representation currently utilized was examined at three sites in the USA:

- The New Museum at the John F. Kennedy Library, Boston, Massachusetts
- The Sixth Floor, John F. Kennedy and the Memory of a Nation, Dallas, Texas
- Arlington National Cemetery, Arlington, Virginia.

The interpretation and re-telling of events surrounding the death have shaped perceptions of reality. In projecting visitors into the past, reality has been replaced with omnipresent simulation and commodification. Thus the real is confined in pure repetition (Baudrillard, 1983).

Central to the interpretation of Kennedy's life, and in particular his death, are pictorial repetitions of such key images as the assassinations of JFK and Lee Harvey Oswald, Jacqueline Kennedy in mourning at the funeral, John (Jnr) Kennedy's salute, the riderless horse, the Walter Cronkite (CBS) news flash intimating the shooting and the eternal flame at Arlington. Such images have become international markers of collective memory. As Knapp (1989) notes, they trigger shared social dispositions relating personal life to the date and time of the assassination. In both the JFK New Museum in Boston and the Sixth Floor in Dallas, media are used as the basis for interpretation. The multiplicity of roles for media in the Kennedy story, contextualizing, telling, promoting and recollecting are central mechanisms in his life. Known as the 'television president' he was believed to be one of the earliest to grasp the political importance of that medium. From the initial 'great debate' with Nixon through the regular live televized news conferences to his ultimatum on US television demanding that Russian missiles be removed from Cuba, he showed an early mastery of TV. Consequently many of the exhibits utilized footage from the critical events of Kennedy's life. Television and film are also clearly linked with the assassination and central to its retelling and interpretation. As White noted: 'Television was at the centre of the shock. With its indelible images, information, immediacy, repetition and close-ups, it served to define the tragedy for the public' (1982, p. 174).

In the USA, TV had rapidly grown as a critically important media for news and by the 1960s some 88 per cent of all homes owned TV sets (White, 1982). Key events where media had an important role included the fateful weekend JFK was assassinated – from the point of the shooting, to the scenes outside the hospital, Johnson's swearing-in, the murder of Lee Harvey Oswald, and the Kennedy funeral. Central and notable in the media coverage was the death itself which offered a spectacle of televisual images defining the 'reality' of that weekend for many viewers. The viewing of the funeral itself constituted the heaviest day of TV viewing in the USA to date with some 93 per cent of TV-equipped households watching the funeral procession to Arlington National Cemetery (Neilsen, 1963). These images, which constituted 'touches of pure television' (*Broadcast Magazine*, 1963, p. 50), have been utilized heavily in both of the attractions examined in Dallas and Boston. The media image of JFK is an enduring one of this period in USA history. Within thirty-six months of JFK's assassination more than two hundred books had been published pertaining to the tragedy. This has been joined by a further 1,000 books, periodical articles, television retrospectives, more than twelve newsletters, and a number of booksellers now specializing in assassination literature (Zelizer, 1992). Indeed, novels and film treatments such as the *The Parallax View, Executive Action* and *JFK*, have all contrived to feed the growing interests in the events of the Kennedy death.[1]

Any 'story' of JFK and review of his presidency will inevitably be affected by these repeated images. Television and film have entered the memory of those events rather than historical data. As Connally (1988) noted:

---

1   See, for example, *JFK*, the celebrated treatment of the Kennedy assassination by Oliver Stone which caused considerable controversy and served to reignite passions some twenty-eight years after the assassination. Furthermore, films centring on related individuals continue to be developed, e.g. *Libra* (1993), a film about Lee Harvey Oswald, and *Ruby* (1992), a film centring on Jack Ruby.

I don't think the time has come when history will really look at the
Kennedy administration with a realistic eye. And how could we?
When you see a beautiful little girl kneeling with her hand on her
father's coffin, when you see a handsome little boy standing with a
military salute by his slain father, how can you feel anything but the
utmost sympathy? It's a scene of pathos, of remorse, of tragedy, and
that's the way we now view President Kennedy.

Cultural authority is herein defined through the narrative pictorial images
clouding historical reality. This process of what Weber called 'rhetorical
legitimation' illustrates how the purveyors of this 'history/story' legitimize
themselves by the stories they tell in discourse with the public. The extent
to which replication of this process occurs in tourist attractions covering
the presidency and assassination of JFK will be considered next.

JFK and the tourist: Boston, Dallas and Washington

The findings and discussion that follow are based upon an examination
of the treatment of JFK in the following locations in the USA:

- the New Museum at the JFK Library, Boston, Massachusetts
- the Sixth Floor, Dallas, Texas
- the Eternal Flame, Arlington National Cemetery, Arlington,
  Virginia.

All sites were visited and participant observation was undertaken.
Interviews were conducted with representatives of local tourist
authorities, museum operators, management and staff and, where
appropriate, local media were examined.

The attractions represent varying approaches to interpreting JFK, the
presidency and the assassination. The *New Museum at the JFK Library,
Boston*, is very much an education and research centre incorporating a
museum which 'portrays the life of John F. Kennedy, traces the career of
his brother Robert F. Kennedy, and illustrates the nature of the office of
the President of the United States' (John F. Kennedy Library, 1994, p. 2).
This is a paid-entrance attraction incorporating an innovative treatment

18   *JFK Library, Boston, Massachusetts*

of the presidency via a trip around a simulated White House layout. The library houses extensive presidential archives which are also open to the public. Essentially this is a museum celebrating the achievements and the life of JFK. There is little in-depth coverage of the darker side of the President's character, administrative failings or weaknesses. Interpretation is in the context of the times. For example, the election trail is interpreted through shop-fronts of the 1950s and the peace corps development is covered through a representation of a White House room incorporating video archive material. Indeed, newsreel and TV footage are central to interpretation of this site. In each of the White House rooms and other locations there are screens located as a primary element of exhibition space. Artefacts and objects on display are not authenticated and it is difficult to know, for example, whether the desk in the Oval Office is the authentic one JFK sat at, or is merely a replica. For a traditional museum in the UK such authentication would be of considerable importance but it is secondary in this museum to the use of TV and newsreel footage which provide the 'reality'. Small TV screens are used to show television clips in an attempt to give the visitor the 'impression' that someone at the time would have had when watching their own TV. The fabric of memory

19   *The Sixth Floor (entrance), Dallas, Texas*

is framed by the TV set. Furthermore, the central role of the media in generating the Kennedy myth is clearly reinforced.

The Sixth Floor, Dallas, Texas, provides another perspective on JFK which will of course remain synonymous with his assassination. This is described as a visitor centre developed by the Dallas County Historical Foundation (Dallas County Historical Federation, 1989) and is a paid attraction located in the former Texas School Book Depository. The visitor centre documentation summarizes the arguments for development as follows:

> It was created to meet the widespread visitor demand for information and understanding about a tragic but important event . . . documentary films and interpretive displays help those who remember come to grips with a powerful memory, and educate younger audiences about the meaning of an unforgettable chapter in American history. (ibid., 1989, p. 2)

This 'permanent historical display on the life, death and legacy of President Kennedy' (Dallas County Historical Foundation, 1994a, p. 5) opened in 1989. The Sixth Floor is operated as a non-profit-making organization and was established in 1983. It is located in the Dealey Plaza district which in 1993 was designated as a National Historical Landmark District. This means the site has been given formal designation by the Federal Government of the USA since the site is believed to be of outstanding historical significance. The site is officially marked very close to the point of the assassination by a plaque in the ground on the north side of Elm Street. As the Sixth Floor press release notes: 'This location makes the plaque easily visible for the majority of visitors and allows for photography' (Dallas County Historical Foundation, 1994d, p. 2). The plaque's wording is curiously circumspect in recording that this is a site commemorating the assassination of a former President of the USA. The plaque simply states the following:

Dealey Plaza
has been designated a
National Historical Landmark.
This site possesses national significance
in commemorating the history of the
United States of America
1993

National Park Service
United States Department of the Interior

(ibid., p. 2)

In 1994 some 420,863 visitors toured the Sixth Floor Museum, making it Dallas' number one paid tourist attraction for the third consecutive year (Dallas County Historical Foundation, 1994e).

The Sixth Floor consists of some 9,000 square feet of exhibition space on the sixth level of the former Texas School Book Depository building. Upwards of four hundred photographs, six documentary films (heavily based on contemporary TV coverage) and a range of artefacts and displays are grouped to chronicle the events from the early 1960s through the assassination and on to the legacy (Dallas County Historical Foundation, 1994f). Publicity for the Sixth Floor notes that, 'No original evidence is on display; all materials in this exhibition are suitable for family viewing' (Dallas County Historical Foundation, 1989, p. 2), presumably a reference to the fact that the exhibition does not include some of the most graphic images in the famous Zapruder film. Yet two 'evidential' areas associated with Lee Harvey Oswald have been reconstructed. These constitute:

1. The corner window – a recreation of the window area from where the assassin's bullet was allegedly fired. The window remains permanently open.
2. The corner staircase – a reconstruction of where the sniper allegedly exited and where the rifle was discovered.

In this way the visitor is projected into the 'authenticated' reality of that period on the day of the assassination.

Recognizing the relatively controversial nature of this 'educational exhibition', the Sixth Floor PR Department has produced a set of questions and answers to justify the development with a reference to JFK's [sic] own words in the following context:

Question: Wouldn't it be better just to leave the subject alone?

Answer: President Kennedy himself said that 'History is the memory of a nation'. History is poorly served by burying the past. New generations of Americans have grown up since 1963, and they have a right to learn more about this important event in their history. Despite the emotions that surround this event, there is a responsibility to face history squarely and to recount it accurately. Democratic societies are expected to interpret all of their history – the tragedies as well as the achievements. (excerpt from *Questions and Answers*, Dallas County Historical Foundation, 1994h, p. 1)

The educative mission of the attraction is continually reiterated along with the historical significance of the location. This whole issue of justification of development constitutes an on-going debate. Similar questions involving the views of the Kennedy family are also broached by the PR Department in the same fact sheet:

Question: Has the Kennedy family been involved in this project?

Answer: Because the museum touches on a personal family tragedy, Dallas County Historical Foundation has never felt it appropriate to ask the Kennedys to become involved in this project or to comment on it. (ibid., p. 2)

More accurately, the Kennedy family have consistently sought to distance themselves from images of the president's death and to attempt to concentrate attention on appraisal of JFK's life. Indeed, the family boycotted certain public memorial services and by the 1970s had begun to avoid commemorative services (Zelizer, 1992). Furthermore, they had called for national commemorations not on 22 November (the date of the assassination) but on JFK's date of birth. Specifically commenting on this development, Senator Edward Kennedy has let it be known that the family were upset that the $3.8m exhibit was being developed at all, but that they would not attempt to halt the opening: 'The family has taken the position that the only memorial should be the Kennedy Library (in Boston), with its outreach capabilities in terms of inspiring people to service' (Edward Kennedy, quoted in Aguirre, 1988, p. 33). Here again, the emphasis on education and the service ethic are reiterated. Indeed, the direct involvement of Jacqueline Kennedy in the final choice of design and location of the JFK Library reinforces that commitment (Reid, 1995). It is interesting to note that the director of the JFK Library in Boston condemned outright the idea of the Sixth Floor development as 'morbid or disgusting, or both' (Daly, quoted in Associated Press, 1988, p. 1).

Since opening in February 1989 the Sixth Floor has received numerous awards, most particularly for its use of video[2] and the quality of the museum, yet support for the development was not immediate in Dallas. The future of the building had been in doubt up until 1977 when the

---

2   This use of video, most particularly TV news of the time (of which six short films are available for sale in video format in the retail store), once again makes explicit the attempts of the media personnel to legitimize themselves as the historians of the period. Through the film coverage of the assassination events in Dallas, the journalists attempt to gain credentials as the purveyors of the historical record (Zelizer, 1992).

county voted to purchase and renovate the building. Its potential for conventional usage was invariably problematic and the county commissioners looked to Dallas County Historical Commission and the Texas Historical Commission for guidance on development (Minutaglia, 1993). In the late 1970s Dallas's major tourist attractions were 'South Fork Ranch' (of *Dallas* TV series fame) and 'Six Flags Over Texas' (a large amusement park). The site of the assassination, although at this stage undeveloped, was still a major draw for visitors since, in many senses, Dallas was defined and identified internationally as the assassination site. The former Texas Book Depository building had remained virtually untouched since 1963 and the site remained practically anonymous without indication or interpretation until the development of the museum over the period 1983 to 1989 and the designation of the site as a National Historical Landmark in 1993. The interpretive development was hotly debated within Texas at a local and state level over a period of eleven years until the project finally opened in 1989. Its 'success' somewhat overshadows the JFK Library which, although twice as large, only barely exceeds the Sixth Floor in terms of visitor numbers. Indeed, the success of the Sixth Floor as a tourist attraction was recognized early on by the Texas Department of Highways and Public Transportation. As the Department's spokesman noted, 'the memorial actually helps Dallas maintain its strong showing as the second most popular city in Texas . . . The bottom line is that we've seen tourists stay in the West End district longer because of the exhibit (Gates, quoted in Read, 1991, p. 7). The commercial benefits of the development are mirrored on a smaller scale in the internal retail outlet which operates within the Sixth Floor. Approximately 200 sq. ft are devoted to the sale of books and Kennedy-related souvenirs. Key rings, pens and T-shirts – all are on offer despite the original intent of the project director Conover Hunt, who stated in 1988 prior to opening that: 'There's no way that anything tacky is going to get into this bookstore . . . There will be no souvenirs coming out of this, it's just not appropriate' (ibid., p. 17).

Commercial orientation extends to the development of corporate membership of the Sixth Floor and evening rental of the facility with corporate hospitality included (Price, 1994). The introduction of catering facilities is currently being debated. Commercial development has to be contrasted with the historical/educative mission which is the justification for development within Dallas and has been linked to the absolution of communal guilt, 'coming to terms' with history and an attempt to align Dallas with other sites of historical tragedy. As the project manager, Conover Hunt, noted:

> Dallas is joining other cities that have had to confront the problem of stewardship of a tragic part of history . . . and like Washington DC, Pearl Harbor, Gettysburg and Manassas [battlefield in northern Virginia], Dallas has dealt with the demand for information by creating a prominent educational display for the public. (Hunt, quoted in Collins, 1989, p. 1B)

Similar attempts at aligning the Sixth Floor with the Ford Theater in Washington (the site of President Lincoln's assassination) and the Lorraine Motel in Memphis (the site of Martin Luther King's assassination) have been made by public policy-makers in the field.[3] Further, this process of alignment was used by the chairman of Dallas Chamber of Commerce to absolve the city and the people of Dallas from any perceived 'communal' guilt. An alignment of Adolf Hitler and Lee Harvey Oswald was made in an interview with the authors:

> Throughout world history there have been people who have abused the power given to them by birthright, circumstance, economic wealth, who have imposed their will on other people whether it is a lone gunman like Lee Harvey Oswald or Adolf Hitler . . . perhaps the two single most evil men of the twentieth century. (Douglas, 1994)

In the context of the assassination, the attribution of blame to a 'lone gunman' is, of course, a political statement rejecting any of the conspiracy theories propounded in a number of books and films. To equate the actions of the (untried) Oswald with those of Adolf Hitler is, to say the least, unusual but recent fieldwork in Germany, Poland and the Czech

---

3   In this case, Richard Sellars, National Parks Service Historian and Chief of the National Park Service, South West Regional Cultural Resource Center, Santa Fe, New Mexico, has compared the Sixth Floor development favourably with the $8.8m project to renovate the Lorraine Motel and establish a National Civil Rights Center. Once again the process of comparison and peer alignment has emerged along with the historical/educative justification for the development of such 'dark' attractions.

20   *The Eternal Flame, Arlington, Virginia*

Republic (see Foley and Lennon, 1995a) suggests that *as tourism 'products'*, similarities can be drawn.

Arlington National Cemetery, Arlington, Virginia – the site of Kennedy's grave and the 'eternal' flame represents a further commodified 'attraction' which has been commercially developed as a part of the Arlington National Cemetery tour. Notable on the tour are isolated stops built around the key burial sites of both John and Robert Kennedy, the *Challenger* space shuttle crew, the grave of Audie Murphy, etc. The 'tour-mobile' bus was a paid narrative tour that took approximately 50 to 60 minutes and allowed tourists to disembark to explore particular grave sites and reboard the bus at a later stage. At the site of the eternal flame tourists were given an explicit instruction that they had '8 minutes for photographs and visits, the next tour bus will be along in approximately thirty minutes' (Arlington Bus Tour, 1994).

What this led to was essentially a scramble to see the grave and have photographs taken at the site. Indeed, this was perhaps the least reverential of all of the Kennedy sites examined.

Locations, celebration and reverence

In any comparison of the Kennedy sites clear differences in production (celebration of achievement in interpretation) and consumption were encountered. Diagram 1 shows the location of sites within a matrix which clearly places the grave site (the eternal flame) as the least reverential behaviour, with the JFK Library clearly illustrating celebration of the life of JFK in a highly uncritical manner and generating reverential behaviour in connection with the assassination. The Sixth Floor, by comparison, is a reverential and respectful treatment of a difficult subject yet it is far less celebratory in its interpretation.

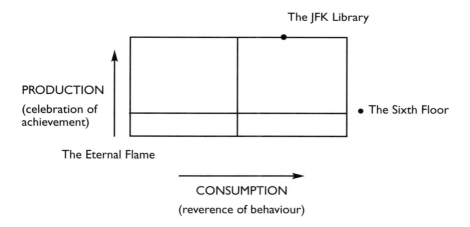

Diagram 1   *Matrix showing treatment of location in terms of production and consumption*

The grave site is invariably different from the museum operations of Boston and Dallas which display and reflect a representation of JFK which is seemingly authoritative. Meaning and 'reality' are conveyed by the 'writer' or 'teller' in both museums, relying heavily on journalistic and televisual interpretation of the events of the presidency and the assassination. These authentic newsreels, assembled by curators and museum professionals, along with text, provide and confer meaning. The television/film image is replayed as the historical 'reality' (Urry, 1990) yet the professionalism of the curator/museum professional is located in the context of a paid attraction in both cases. Financial imperatives and the need for economic efficiency drive the provision of elements such as retailing and catering (Walsh, 1992; Lennon and McPherson, 1995). In this respect the past, be it tragic or celebratory, is commodified in interpretation and becomes a site of commodity consumption. The commodification is illustrated well in the development of the logo for the Sixth Floor – a single red band among the other seven floors of the symbolic building. Carefully, a Kennedy/assassination tag has been avoided in the corporate image. Yet this is clearly locating the 'recent past' in the visitor attraction market place. The logo representation is utilized on merchandise throughout the retail outlet to establish identity and generate revenue. It is a corporate logo for a commercial operation.

The justification for both museums is frequently cited as jointly popularity and educational mission. Yet popularity is no justification of acceptability and cannot be equated with quality. Similarly, the educative mission of both attractions veers very closely towards spectacle (cf. Walsh, 1992). Furthermore, the heavy dependence upon newsreel for interpretive purposes reveals a fundamental difficulty of delineating education and entertainment/spectacle and an uncritical approach to history. The criteria of education quality, critical insight and academic credibility were mainly cited by project directors, managers and curators as central to their 'missions'. Yet what is happening is that the past is being manipulated and relabelled to convey a tourism/leisure orientation (Rojek, 1993b). Arlington National Cemetery with its narrated bus tour and walking map is a further example of this repositioning. As Rojek comments:

> Bourgeois culture invented certain spaces and signs with an 'auratic' quality. The individual was required to relate to them with gravity, respect and sobriety. If the cemetery provides us with the ideal example it is because of its physical size in the landscape of modernity and its elective affinity with the sacred in bourgeois culture. Who, in bourgeois culture, would have dreamt of allowing the cemetery to become a tourist attraction? (ibid., p. 170)

It is part of the process of de-differentiation in post-modern culture. Urry (1990) questions whether it is possible to develop a museum/heritage centre preserving any set of objects in a particular location anywhere in the world. Yet location has significance in both historical/geographical contexts for the sites considered in this book with perhaps the JFK Library's location in the Kennedy heartland of Boston, Massachusetts, being the most tenuous. Museums such as the Sixth Floor strike associations with the past, a key historical personality of the twentieth century, and also with a 'darker' aspect of tourism.

As the Marketing Director of the Sixth Floor, Dallas, Texas, reflected on the nature of the Sixth Floor as a tourist attraction:

> No one wants to come here and see, I hope, a re-hash enactment of the Kennedy assassination. They want to be able to experience it safely knowing that it's over and done, even though our particular box may not be very neat but it's in a package, and you can look at it, and you can feel it, but if it hurts too much it's not happening now so you can put those pieces back. (Price, 1994)

The dilemma of development: the Sixth Floor, Dallas, Texas

The development of the Sixth Floor presented Dallas politicians with a major dilemma that encouraged extensive debate and consideration of alternative use of the building. What the city now possesses is a major attraction and the main reason for visitors entering the fashionable West End Historical District (Herrera, 1994). Recording approximately 0.5 million paying visitors a year this remains Dallas's premier paid attraction with an average annual increase of visitors in excess of 15 per cent. Attendance fluctuations are noted during times of media focus on any aspect of the Kennedy story. For example, the release of Oliver Stone's controversial *JFK* motion picture and the recent thirtieth anniversary commemorations of the assassination correlate directly to increases in visitor attendance (Dallas County Historical Foundation, 1994e).

Yet this was not always the case and initially the building was seen as more of a negative legacy than a potential attraction. The School Book Depository building in Dallas, Texas, left Dallas County State legislators with a dilemma. After the assassination, the building was clearly a difficult real estate proposition and state employees were understandably less than enthusiastic working on the sixth level (from which Oswald had allegedly fired the fatal shots). At the time of the President's death the building was owned by a Dallas industrialist and leased to the school authority for book storage. The School Book Depository was relocated in mid-1971, leaving the building empty. Yet it remained in private ownership, further complicating any intervention by state or city authorities as an acceptable alternative utilization of the building. Yet, as early as 1968, the initial proposal to develop a historical museum to 'maintain and preserve all elements pertaining to the assassination' (McKool, quoted in Calhoun, 1968, p. 1) had been proposed. However, disagreements over funding meant that progress on such a development was slow. The State legislature were unwilling to release funds for what was considered a city project (ibid.). The building was owned by Colonel D. Harold Byrd who had leased the building to the Texas School Book Depository Company (a textbook brokerage firm). The development of a Kennedy assassination museum was seen as an alternative to the city's initial form of commemoration. This constituted a modernist stone cenotaph located in the city some five minutes walk from Dealey Plaza. This monument, known as the Kennedy Memorial, was constructed with $200,000 worth of public contributions from the people of Dallas. It was designed by Philip Johnson and, over the years, its stark appearance came to be seen as increasingly unsatisfactory, by authorities and policy-makers, as a fitting final memorial to the President. It was deliberately located some distance from the death site and for some legislators provided an acceptable level of investment in the memory of the assassination.

However, the proposed museum did not at this stage progress to reality and the development failed because of the lack of available finance. In April 1970 the building was sold to Aubrey Mayhew of Nashville, Tennessee, who proposed to move the contents of his Nashville Museum of John F. Kennedy Memorabilia, to the Texas Schoolbook Depository Building and form a new museum of this historical location. Despite the slow progress of the commercial developers since the assassination (in 1963) the building had become an attraction (albeit undeveloped) for many visitors to the city. According to press reports of the time it was 'ogled daily by hundreds of camera-toting Dallas sightseers' (Kleiwer and Martin, 1991, p. 1). Mayhew's plans were ambitious, utilizing floors one to five, leaving the sixth dramatically empty [sic]. Mayhew was keen to promote the development as an 'historically significant' national museum and not a 'tourist trap' (Mayhew, quoted in Kleiwer and Martin, 1971, p. 1). Here, then, came one of the first defences of the exploitation of the building for historical and learning purposes.

Mayhew's development proposal never materialized since he also was unable to obtain financial support for his ideas. Following default on loan repayment and an arson attack on the building, the building reverted back to Byrd in 1972. Byrd was unable to sell it and by 1977 Dallas County administration were given the option of purchasing. In 1977 this was done by a 2–1 majority of the County who voted to buy and renovate the building known as the Texas School Book Depository as a museum (Dallas County Historical Foundation, 1995c). Over this period, a relatively vociferous lobby within Dallas had argued for the demolition of the building and re-landscaping of the whole area, but the city refused to issue a demolition permit and made a decision to locate the county government in floors one to five of the building with the Sixth Floor to be developed as a museum. Thus the city authorities provided the alternative to commercial operators who had over a period of almost fifteen years consecutively failed to raise finances for the project.

Dallas County Historical Commission were appointed to oversee the development of the museum. This non-profit-making organization now operates the 'attraction'. The conversion cost for the Sixth Floor was estimated at $3 million with the majority of development costs coming from private donations. The operating costs of the museum were to be covered by the revenue-generating aspects such as admission, audio tour hire and retail (Hoppe, 1982).

The development was justified to the media and interested parties in terms of a latent demand from visitors to Dallas to have a Kennedy-related experience. As Conover Hunt-Jones (Director of the Dallas County Historical Foundation) noted:

People will continue to come to Dallas because it will be passed on that Kennedy was a great man. And there will be reverence for him. I think our obligation in Dallas is to accommodate that need in an accurate, tasteful, sensitive manner, deal with it, and then go on in creating an international city. (Hunt-Jones, quoted in Geddie, 1983, p. 1)

The Sixth Floor development occurred at the same time as Dallas was positioning itself as an international tourist and convention destination. Yet this was to prove to be a far from advantageous coincidence. The interest in Dealey Plaza remained considerable with an average of 300 people per day visiting the site on Elm Street where Kennedy was shot (Hunt-Jones, ibid.).

The museum fund-raising ran into difficulties since there was wide-scale reluctance on the part of corporate donors to commit. Many felt that association with the development could be potentially negative for company image and profile both nationally and internationally. Indeed, from its initial set-up in 1982 until early 1986 the fund-raising panel proved spectacularly unsuccessful in terms of generating interest and stimulating corporate sponsorship (Miller, 1985, p. 1A). Part of the difficulty for Conover Hunt-Jones and her team was that fund-raising was occurring at an embarrassing time for the city. As the chairman of the fund-raising foundation noted on the low level of success in the early 1980s: 'In the early '80s the city was putting on its best face for the Republican Convention in 1984 . . . At that time there was a natural reluctance to recall a dark period in the city's history' (Hunt, quoted in Dallas County Historical Foundation, 1995f). What is interesting is the way in which fund-raising for the museum and development of the city was rationalized by the developers depending on the context of the discussion. Indeed, it was not until 1987 when the city itself moved in to fill the funding gap that construction and development could begin. Dallas County sold $2.2 million worth of revenue bonds to pay for the construction of the external elevator tower. That amount formed a 'soft' (low interest) loan that is being currently repaid from admission income.

Significant resistance to the whole project still persisted at the city level. The Dallas Historic Preservation League was most audible and vociferous in its condemnation of the development. As its chairman commented: 'It's a disgrace, like the city is exploiting Kennedy's death . . . it's blood and gore and distasteful. A lot of people are very upset about the whole thing' (Wurmstedt, 1987, p. 1.1) Earlier in the 1970s a group by the name of Dallas Onward had campaigned openly for the demolition of the building arguing that it could never be a memorial to Kennedy, only to Lee Harvey Oswald. Yet despite this in the following decade the county funding of the project was increased to $8 million for the development.

Clearly, the city administration view was to progress the development. Thus the educative/memorial/healing mission and purpose continually reiterated by curators and staff must be seen in the context of an administration keen to capitalize on the 'dark' interest evidenced at a site of assassination. As an attraction, policy-makers at a city level were keen it should operate as a stand-alone facility that would at the very least recoup development costs. As County Judge Lee Jackson commented in the debate on admission charges:

> Dallas County is not going into the historical exhibition business . . . This program will not be supported by tax dollars unless someone on the Commissioners Court wants to change the financing. We all agreed the exhibit would pay for itself. (Jackson, quoted in Young, 1988, p. 2)

Yet simultaneously the educative mission was also stressed by the same administration in public defence of the development. As one newspaper commentary from the administration noted, 'the display will be an educational exhibit, not a museum. No artefacts, such as guns or clothes, will be present' (ibid., p. 1.1). Similarly, the retail outlet was to represent a carefully planned and sensitively stocked facility offering educational rather than souvenir items (Martin, 1988). Yet commercial pressures have clearly repositioned the original orientation. Mugs, pencils and videos of media treatments of the assassination can be found in the 200 square foot retail outlet. Whilst postcards are currently not on offer the bookshop does sell a novel volume entitled *John F. Kennedy and his Family: Paper Dolls in Full Colours*, a cut-out child's book which allows the reader to dress and undress John F. Kennedy, Jackie and the children (Bull, 1995). Its educative mission is clearly compromised. A local vendor offered a more forthright view on the role of souvenirs, such as the Dealey Plaza postcard (with assassination spot indicated): 'I get a lot of negative reaction to it, but I do it because it's history . . . The public when they go to a historic site, want something to buy, a memento or something to remember the trip' (Wade, quoted in Martin, 1988, p. 7).

Since opening, the Sixth Floor financial performance has been publicly praised by local administrators who choose to focus on operational costs and contributions to overheads rather than the historical or educational aspects. As County Budget Director Scheps noted after the exhibit opened to capacity crowds:

> The exhibit's popularity will continue to grow, generating a $500,000 nest egg by the year 2000, when the exhibit's debt will be repaid. Based on existing entrance fees and operating costs, the exhibit thereafter could generate between $300,000 and $400,000 a year . . . the historical foundation is running the exhibit well and paying their bill. Meanwhile there's been no deterioration in public interest with the exhibition. (Scheps, quoted in Martin, 1991)

The commercial operation was also linked to the potential preservation of buildings that it could stimulate in the Dallas 'historic' West End. This is the now developed district tourist area of shops and themed restaurants in which the Book Depository building is located. As the Director of the Dallas County Historical Foundation argued, the Sixth Floor would provide an anchor site which would provide 'a permanent source of revenue to help the county prevent history from simply disappearing' (Hays, quoted in Martin, 1991).

The clear commercial orientation evidenced in public discussion of the Sixth Floor is ironically refuted in various Dallas County Historical Museum press releases, for example, the 'questions and answers' press release considers the tourist attraction operation as follows:

Question: Is the museum intended to be a tourist attraction?

Answer: The museum is a non-commercial project and has not been created to draw tourists to the site of the assassination. They are already there.

Yet the Sixth Floor brochure is mailed to 'all hotel information centers, Dallas Convention Business Bureau information centers, state border points and everywhere we can get it' (Price, Marketing Director – Sixth

Floor – interview analysis, 1996). Once again, the reality of marketing is evident in what is a clearly commercial product. Such commercial arrangements have to be contrasted with the Director quoted later in the same article who justifies the whole development by reference to claims of inherent public demand:

> The only reason the exhibit is here is because of an overwhelming public demand . . . No one was satisfied with that empty cenotaph, which just signified an absence. They wanted to connect with the experience in some way. So, we gave them something tasteful. (Hays, quoted in Martin, 1991)

The extent of demand had grown to a worldwide phenomenon by 1995 when the press release fact sheet noted the Sixth Floor Museum was organized 'in response to this worldwide educational demand' (Dallas County Historical Foundation, 1994f, p. 1). Clearly, ambivalence about purpose, haste and even focus of this site is part of the administrators' and policy-makers' relativism which is continually being reapplied in respect of this site.

This site remains Dallas's number one paid attraction and according to some estimates the most visited attraction in Northern Texas (Minutaglia, 1993). This statistic is echoed by the president of Dallas Visitor and Convention Bureau who went further, identifying the Sixth Floor as a 'marketing tool' for the city of Dallas (Herrera interview analysis, 1996).

The site may develop further (following its success in visitor numbers) and there is now discussion of an archive centre on the seventh floor. Furthermore, any redevelopment of the surrounding area is monitored very closely by the Dallas County Historical Foundation. A proposal to site a DART (Rapid Transit City Railway) station in the parking lot near to the Sixth Floor and location of the 'second' gunman has evoked strong resistance. As the Dallas County Historical Foundation project director responded: 'It would be like building railroad tracks across the Gettysburg National Battlefield' (Hunt, quoted in Posey, 1988, p. 22). Such an over-reaction may be driven more by commercial loss rather than curatorial motivation.

The last steps – from simulacra to re-enactment

The final development of the Dealey Plaza site has to be the 'JFK Presidential Limousine Tour' which over a period of one hour travels from Love Field Airbase to the assassination point on Elm Street. For $25.00 visitors retrace the route in a replica of the presidential limousine, with an audio commentary playing on the car tape deck that includes crowd cheers, gunshot sounds, comments of other passengers (e.g. Governor John Connolly) and the news broadcast covering the death of the President. The tour culminates in a rapid drive to Portland Hospital where the experience terminates with confirmation of the President's death (Murray, 1996). For the post-emotional society this type of re-enactment with 'real-time' commentary offers the closest one can come to reliving events. It constitutes a logical progression from the Sixth Floor and is illustrative of the extent to which Dallas city authorities have relaxed their attitude to more overt forms of exploitation of the assassination.

CHAPTER SEVEN

War Sites of the First and Second World Wars

The landscapes of both Belgium and France were battlegrounds in the First and Second World Wars, events which had a critical role in shaping the political economy of Europe since 1918, as well as becoming key elements in the history and other curricula in many European schools' examination systems. It is inconceivable that any EC citizen could be unaware of the substantives of these events, whether through personal experience of 'total war', through numerous cinematic, documentary and literary efforts or via the ways in which these are used to develop an understanding of heritage through history in schools and colleges throughout the region. Many citizens of the EC and of other Allied nations, notably Canada and the USA, have memories of fighting in the conflicts of Western Europe, or lost friends or family members during these wars. The evidence of conflict looms large over some parts of the landscape and urban architecture of Belgium and France (as it does in several parts of the remainder of Europe), with battle sites, cemeteries, memorials, buildings, emplacements, bunkers, museums and interpretative facilities forming significant parts of land-use in some regions.

Such resources – both physical and those of personal and collective memory – are, we have argued, critical to the development of a tourist product associated with dark tourism. In the cases of Belgium and France, the opportunities of tourism are reinforced by a political imperative concerned with portrayal of events which had fundamental consequences for the re-establishment of modern Europe along 'rational' political and economic lines after 1945. It is worth adding here that, of course, the bombing of London, Coventry or Clydebank were also significant events of the Second World War which contributed to the landscape and architecture of Britain, and that similar analogies could be constructed for almost any nation–state involved in that conflict. Our concern here is not to elevate the significance of events upon Belgium and France, but to examine the growth of a significant tourism product which has arisen around the landscape, hardware and memory of war in these countries.

The particular characteristics of the First and Second World Wars which have attracted the tourism industries are, themselves, worth considering. It is suggested that, for a number of reasons, those aspects which have been attractive in Belgium and France are dissimilar from other sites associated with these conflicts elsewhere, and this chapter begins with a brief overview of the wars and a review of issues arising from some well-established tourist sites which represent these wars outside Belgium and France – the sites of Nazi concentration camps have been deliberately excluded from this analysis as these are considered elsewhere in this book. It continues with a detailed consideration of some key sites and experiences available in Belgium and France and ends with some observations upon the implications for the concept of dark tourism.

The First and Second World Wars and their significance for dark tourism

For most schoolchildren, the origins of the First World War are tied to ideas of the failure of diplomacy, the escalation of an 'arms race', the end of Britain's 'splendid isolation' and the concomitant proliferation of interlinking treaties bringing responsibilities to protect the sovereignty of some when compromised by others. The volatility of the Balkans region provided the spark (the assassination of the Archduke Ferdinand of Austria–Hungary in Sarajevo by Gavrilo Princip) which ignited a series of events culminating in the mobilization of Germany's Schlieffen Plan for invasion of Belgium and France. On the western side of Europe the invasion of Belgium and the obligation upon Britain to maintain Belgium's neutrality brought Britain into the conflict, first by the despatch of a regular army in the form of the British Expeditionary Force. The inability of that force to end the conflict by Christmas 1914 set in train a series of events in which Belgium and much of France was occupied by Germany and the British: French and German armies faced each other across a series of trenches, stretching effectively from Switzerland to the sea. Trench warfare with horrific casualties in terms of numbers and types of injuries, commanded by staff officers domiciled miles from the front and effected by conscript armies and junior officers in conditions of appalling privations, became the 'norm' until 1917, with occasional attempts by either side to break through the other's trenches sufficiently to gain significant advantage – usually frustrated and with enormous casualties for the attacking side. From the point of view of Britons, this war of attrition was being conducted on foreign soil and largely away from any immediate impact upon them – albeit, numbers of casualties and social changes associated with a war economy were evident throughout the land – aside from a small number of Zeppelins which reached parts of the UK. Elsewhere, other nations were involved in equally bloody conflict, again shaping the landscape and life of these societies and economies. The USA, which remained neutral until 1917, escaped the significant negative effects of the war – with no violation of its territories or significant loss of citizens' lives. Having joined the conflict in Europe in 1917, the addition of USA troops, together with a successful blockade of Germany and agitation in German cities, contributed to a final onslaught which ended in an Allied victory in Europe (and ultimately, elsewhere). The war had ravaged the landscape of great parts of Belgium and France, destroyed major parts of some cities, towns and villages and all but brought economic activity to a standstill. Britain, Canada, France, Russia, Germany and others had lost huge numbers of young men in the conflict and all faced economic problems at home.

It is often argued that the Second World War arose from the failure to adequately resolve the end of the First, whether via the introduction of punitive reparations and territory changes upon the ailing German economy or upon the failure to secure an adequately effective League of Nations. Equally, economic problems worldwide in the interwar years meant that Germany was not alone in its difficulties, and the political implications of Bolshevism, arising from the Russian Revolution of 1917, troubled many governments.

Despite policies of appeasement aimed at preventing a war with Hitler, the inevitable happened in 1939 when Europe was, once again, plunged into war with the occupation of France. The establishment of a Vichy government there as Nazi 'puppets', the evacuation of British troops from Dunkirk in 1940, and the spectacular successes of German armies in occupying most of Western Europe, other than Britain and the subsequent 'Battle of Britain', brought a significant focus of activities around the coastline of Europe and Britain. The bombing of cities by both sides and the inevitable civilian casualties brought a new dimension of terror to warfare which had not previously been apparent – that innocent, non-military citizens became directly involved in the conflict and, accordingly, acquired a strategic significance. Civilian casualties were inevitable in earlier wars, but these were often accidental, incidental or tactical acts of terror, rather than strategic considerations for the conduct of war. The consolidation of an 'Atlantic Wall' along the coastline of mainland Europe by the Axis forces intended to rebuff the anticipated attempt to land troops for a re-invasion by the Allies was a key feature of German strategy in the post-1941 period. The inevitability of an attempted invasion arose from the entry of the USA into the conflict after 1941 when Japanese aircraft attacked the USA Pacific naval base at Pearl Harbor in Honolulu, Hawaii, causing many casualties and the loss of several ships. The Allied invasion, when it came, was meticulously planned and focused upon the long, flat beaches of Normandy in Northern France which were well fortified but were taken by a combination of surprise, speed and strategic planning. Despite considerable casualties in securing the beaches and pushing inland, these D-Day landings provided the basis for a re-occupation of Europe and, ultimately, 'Victory in Europe' when Berlin was captured simultaneously by American, British and Russian troops in an event which heralded and anticipated the 'Cold War' of 1945 to 1979. In other theatres of war, victory for the Allies took longer and, in a war in which technological innovation had become a key element of strategic advantage, the USA government took the decision to precipitate a Japanese surrender and reduce the certain casualties involved in fighting a Pacific War island by island. This involved dropping atomic bombs upon the cities of Hiroshima and Nagasaki with massive consequences of destruction and death for Japanese citizens and upon the collective consciousness of all subsequent generations worldwide.

Thus, taken together, these conflicts have defined the political, economic, technological and social circumstances of the world since 1945. While Europe was neither alone, or even special, in experiencing these postwar effects, it had been the theatre of many wars and would continue with parts of North America via NATO and the Security Council of the UN to play a significant part in shaping the world order. One significant effect was the resurrection of an active concept of Europe, first, via the 'Common Market' and later politically and culturally, encapsulated in Gorbachev's celebrated phrase of a 'common European home'. As the cradle of modernity and the originator of its 'project', Europe holds considerable sway over intellectual life and the promotion of ideas. If a post-modern world can be posited, then it is from Europe that these ideas have emerged, even where the focus of the analysis has been elsewhere on the planet. Thus Europe and its postwar re-emergence shaped by experiences of war, political dichotomy, economic uncertainty and intellectual influence, are both interesting and essential for an understanding of late capitalism. Similarly, transnational tourism, especially cultural tourism, in the postwar period was spearheaded in Europe (as it had been before), and the sights of Europe became attractive and relatively inexpensive to those from North America as technologies originating in the war enabled safe and rapid international travel. Many visitors to Europe were of a generation which had either fought in these wars or had lost friends and relatives in it. Thus, remembrance and the visitation of death sites for this purpose were factors in the desire of some local and central governments to ensure that cemeteries and graves were well tended.

The War in the Pacific

A feature of dark tourism as outlined in earlier chapters has been the difficulty of establishing objective accounts and analyses of the kinds of events which can lead to a dark tourism product. This section considers some situations where the roles of 'victim', 'aggressor', 'winner' and 'loser' become difficult to define. In turn, this can lend a political and ideological element to the interpretations of events, sites and objects which invites controversy and, even, revisionism.

21   USS Arizona *Memorial, Pearl Harbor, Honolulu, Hawaii*

Among the most controversial events of the Second World War have been those which began, and ended, the war for the USA – i.e. the Japanese attack upon Pearl Harbor and the dropping of atom bombs upon the cities of Hiroshima and Nagasaki. These events are commemorated in their respective locations and represent significant opportunities for visitation.

Pearl Harbor is located in Honolulu, Hawaii – a major location of inbound tourism, attracting some 6.5 million visitors per annum. The attack on Pearl Harbor (subject of the film, *Tora, Tora, Tora*) is remembered via the USS *Arizona* Memorial, dedicated in 1962 after appeals for public subscriptions across the USA. When completed, the *Arizona* was one of the most powerful battleships in the world, representing a significant technological achievement and crewed by a complement of over 1,000 men. It was lost in the first minutes of the Japanese attack and although significant armouries and other items were salvaged throughout the war, the ship itself lay below the waterline but close to the surface as it does today. Following various attempts to establish war memorials in the Pacific, a memorial was erected across the sunken wreck in Pearl Harbor and a Visitor Center was established on land, close by. Both the Memorial and the Visitor Center are administered and run by the National Parks Service. A visit to the site is free, but carefully managed. Visitors are allocated a ticket which allows them to enter a cinematic interpretation of the events leading up to the attack, as well as images of the *Arizona* and from the attack itself. Only after seeing the interpretative film is it possible to join small craft crewed by sailors which ply the half-mile between the Visitor Center and the Memorial, which is in the harbour itself – still a working military base. No part of the Memorial touches the ship which lies sunk in 40 feet of water and reverence is encouraged by staff present upon the Memorial structure. Beach-style clothing is not permitted upon the Memorial. The ship is clearly visible below the water and a viewing well enables visitors to drop flowers onto the vessel's starboard side. Thin films of fuel oil rise perpetually to the surface, a matter which is carefully pointed out to visitors. At the far end of the Memorial, a Shrine Room records the names of the 1,117 who perished abroad the ship. Visitors (about 150 at any one time) are required to leave aboard the next-arriving small craft from the shoreside.

The Visitor Center prides itself in presenting both sides of the 'Pearl Harbor story'. When the National Parks Service took over the sites from the US Navy in 1980, it moved to replace the interpretative film then in use, described by the superintendent as a 'Hollywood creation' – in which a fictitious attack upon Pearl Harbor was filmed using American planes – with original film footage, stills and a desire to make it 'as authentic as possible'. According to the superintendent, the theme presented by the Navy had been 'always be prepared' and that this attitude needed to be updated in time for the fiftieth anniversary in 1992 (representing, as it did, a Cold War mindset) with a reflection upon how a nation should remember those who have made the ultimate sacrifice, in a sombre, rather than aggressive, mood. In his words, visitors will go out to the Memorial with 'the proper attitude, as opposed to, "this is just another tourist attraction"'. The *Honolulu Star-Bulletin* reported this change on 3 December 1992 (p. 7) under the banner 'New December 7 Film Debuts at *Arizona*. The Old One Was Criticized as Being Soft on the Enemy'. The article reminds readers that one of the lines in the old film described Admiral Yamamoto (commander of the Japanese forces) as a 'brilliant strategist' and repeated claims that 'visitors from Japan often applauded when the film ended'. A key element of the new film is said to be narration by a female, thereby 'toning down emotions raised by the subject' according to the article.

A key part of the manner of interpretation is based upon the National Parks Service management of several areas of mortal conflict. 'We've learned, you don't take sides, you don't moralize, you tell what happened from a historical perspective. And we do that here [Pearl Harbour] too. We just say, "here's the people involved, here's what happened, when it happened, how it happened, why it happened. You can draw your own moral conclusions"' (all quotations from an interview with Don Magee, Superintendent, July 1995). Of course, the ability to draw these moral conclusions is not informed by the well-established, if empirically dubious, revisionist assertions that President Roosevelt knew of the impending attack but failed to inform the American people or to take evasive action.

Whatever the particular realities of relating an event like the attack upon Pearl Harbor and the inevitability of extending some moral consequence to the act, its precursors and its subsequent representation, the Memorial and Visitor Center have not been without controversy. Some of these are inevitable – the Memorial lies in a working harbour in which it is difficult to delineate reverential and non-reverential space, perhaps more than on land. It is also not the only sacred space in the harbour area, not the only memento of the attack – some buildings retain bullet holes as physical evidence of the attack. Thus, according to Linenthal (1993, p. 192), 'Various attempts have been made to lessen the risk of defilement by building or maintaining both physical and ideological boundaries around the memorial and its message'. Defilement for some has been associated with the presence of Japanese tourists – and Japanese items in gift shops, too many Japanese-made cars in the car parks or Asian American staff who are asked aggressively if they are Japanese. Some go further in their condemnations, for example, the *Star-Bulletin* article of 16 October 1990 highlights the efforts of an individual (A. N. Room) to draw the attention of the US Department of the Interior to what he considers to be the revisionist and biased treatment at the Memorial and Visitor Center. The article paraphrases the complainant by adding that '(he) complains that by not assigning culpability for the attack on Dec. 7, 1941, the Arizona

Memorial rangers may be skewing history in order to cater for Japanese tourists and investors' (*Star-Bulletin*, 1990). The article goes on to say that Room argues that 'by inference, we were as much to blame for Pearl Harbor as the Japanese'. Thus, the lack of moral judgement is itself seen to be an ideological position which sits uncomfortably with some Americans. *The Honolulu Advertiser* (6 December 1993 – 52 years after the attack) asserted that 'some visitors find it hard to forgive' and quotes one, Barry Zucker, as saying that in looking at the rusted wreck of the *Arizona*, he felt two emotions – sorrow for the dead and resentment for the Japanese visitors next to him, thinking that it was 'kind of sacrilegious' that they were at the site. Others in the same article objected to a Japanese (later revealed to be an American of Chinese ancestry) tour guide at the memorial, which one visitor called 'offensive'. As Magee put it in his interview with us, 'They want blame. We said, "certainly you can place your own blame, here's the facts – you draw you own moral conclusions".'

22   USS Arizona *Memorial Museum, Pearl Harbor, Honolulu, Hawaii*

Critical to an understanding of the USS *Arizona* Memorial and Visitor Center are recognitions of a global tourism industry which, inevitably, will bring into contact those formerly in conflict and raise questions of cultural relativity. The role and actions of the Imperial Japanese government and its soldiers during the Second World War, its refusal to apologize for these actions and the hardened attitudes of servicemen, servicewomen, their families and their representative organizations contrast sharply with behaviour at, and reactions to, sites and acts associated with the Jewish Holocaust or the Third Reich in general. This is not to say that there is not anti-German feeling, but rather that there appears to be some separation of contemporary Germany from Nazi Germany, and Nazi acts of brutality. Other sites at which Allied personnel suffered at the hands of the Japanese demonstrate similar reactions – for example, the small chapel at Changi Gaol in Singapore contains many vitriolic messages from visitors aimed at Japan in general and which indicate an absence of any healing or chronological distancing having taken place. Similar strong emotion is observable at the 'Bridge over the River Kwai', in Thailand. Commonly, these sites have far less merchandising (or more discreet, in some cases) than some others mentioned in this book. At Pearl Harbor, the store is a 'book store' which does not sell '. . . lots of schlock. You don't see glasses that show the boat, you don't see drinking cups, anything like that' (interview with Superintendent Don Magee, 1995). Perhaps not surprisingly, other nearby enterprises have sought to fill that market demand.

The events of the end of the war with Japan have proved to be equally problematical for Americans (and Japanese). When the Smithsonian Institute in Washington cancelled its proposed exhibition entitled 'The Last Act: The Atomic Bomb and the End of World War II' in February 1995, veterans' groups claimed a victory for their perspective upon these events. The proposed exhibition had been criticized for questioning why the bomb had been dropped, rather than relying on official statements issued in 1945 which, broadly, indicate that it was used to end the war quickly and to save further casualties, and for attributing the legacy of the Cold War and nuclear arms proliferation to the decision. The Smithsonian agreed to changes in the exhibition, resulting in criticism from historians that 'known facts' were being ignored and that the exhibition was being 'historically cleansed'. As Linenthal puts it, '[Each] side believed that the other had stolen history, resulting either in a revisionist exhibit, dishonoring American veterans or in one showing a callous disregard for historical integrity' (1995a). The resulting exhibition of the fuselage of the aircraft 'Enola Gay' has been discussed earlier in this book. Similar recourse to technological detail in the face of moral dubiety is evident in the US Army Chemical Corps Museum at Fort McClellan, Anniston, Alabama (see Thompson, 1992) which rationalizes developments by US forces in chemical warfare since 1917 while explaining why the US Government has never signed any international accord banning the use of such weapons, asserting that 'The Army continues to stand as a staunch deterrent to the use of weapons of mass destruction by those who would choose them to further their aggressive goals' (US Army Chemical Corps Museum, no date). The museum, which is freely open to visitors Monday to Friday, strives to 'provide information to engender goodwill and promote relations between the US Army and the civilian community' (ibid.) and contains a shop selling a wide range of ceramics, jewellery, gift items, clothing, books and children's items. Significantly, the use of defoliants such as Agent Orange and other chemical weapons in Asian conflicts in the second half of the twentieth century receive scant, if any, attention.

We have alluded to the tension between the commemorative and the historical voice in dark tourism elsewhere (Foley and Lennon, 1997) as well as to the concerns which arise when historical discourse enters a tourism arena. The inevitable revisions which discussion and analysis bring, sometimes associated with significant anniversaries, appear to be a key element of dark tourism, often where distrust of government (whether liberal-democratic or otherwise) is apparent or 'official versions' predominate, such as in interpretations of the Second World War in the former Warsaw Pact countries.

When applied to sites in Japan, which were not visited by the authors of this book, there are apparent criticisms that similar distrust of government could be applied to any future analysis. In reporting the opening of the Nagasaki Atomic Bomb Museum, the Singapore-based *Straits Times* (23 March 1996), suggests that the small section of the museum devoted to Japan's role in the occupation of Asia during 1931 to 1945 and atrocities towards the Chinese and Koreans may represent a significant change in the way that Japanese museums interpret these events. However, and ominously given the above, the Museum Director is reported as making it 'clear that the section will state only the facts of World War II, and not comment on Japan's aggression. The museum, with a strong section on nuclear deterrence, hopes to be objective'. Whatever the success of this museum in achieving objectivity, the *Straits Times* comments that any contextuality concerning Japan's conduct during the war is 'noticeably absent' in the Hiroshima Peace Memorial Museum. In a similar vein, *The Boston Globe* of 24 June 1995, reporting on events which commemorated the fiftieth anniversary of Okinawa, draws attention to

> [the] extreme differences between the war's legacies in Europe and Asia . . . In Europe, 50th anniversary observances have concluded amid scenes of abiding harmony among former foes. In Asia, international relations, domestic politics and personal affairs still are upset frequently by wounds deeply felt, but seldom discussed.

In such circumstances interpretation based upon recognition of history as discourse, as opposed to history as 'objective truth', seems to possess possibilities which are yet culturally alien with regard to the Pacific conflict.

War in England and Germany

This section considers the role played by memorial to, and interpretation of, war in the tourism products of two areas – SE England and the area in and around Berlin. These sites became especially important when the fiftieth anniversaries of the bombing of Dresden, the liberation of Nazi concentration camps, of VE Day, the bombings of Hiroshima and Nagasaki and VJ Day were commemorated worldwide. These commemorations involved large numbers of people visiting and, in some cases returning to, significant sites of the Second World War. In short, these anniversaries involved 'tourism'.

Commentators upon cultural tourism (see Foley, 1995) often point to tensions between 'popular' and 'elite' culture in the tourism product.

The case studies in this section show that in one segment of cultural tourism, which we call dark tourism, the distance between these polar points is often reduced, whether explicitly in techniques of interpretation, or implicitly in the values of retailing and merchandising adopted at ancillary facilities.

Cities have been strategic targets throughout the history of warfare, both as seats of political power and decision-making and as resources for invading forces. Since the Spanish Civil War, the significance of terrorizing civilian populations and disabling economic activity by attacking cities in wartime has become a commonplace of twentieth-century armed conflicts. Many cities suffer the effects of war and some attempt to interpret events in which their citizens have been the targets of attack or their leaders have planned campaigns intended to affect the course of war. From Honolulu to Hiroshima and from Saigon to Singapore conflicts of the twentieth century are offered as part of touristic fare, most often as (ostensibly, at least) a salutary warning that whatever is being represented should never happen again. It is not unusual for parties of schoolchildren from home and abroad to be seen at sites of infamy, degradation and death alongside the elderly on coach tours, historians on theme vacations and the merely curious on a day trip or extended tour.

Beside the Martin-Gropius-Bau in Berlin, a large, undeveloped piece of land is the site of many of the former administrative headquarters of the Nazi repressive state apparatus, including the Gestapo and the SS, *inter alia*. Various interpretative maps on site show the locations of these offices and some ruins and foundations are visible. The site also houses a low flat building which contains 'The Topography of Terrors' permanent exhibition. This exhibition, prepared for the 750th anniversary celebration of the city of Berlin, provides information, through photographs and original texts, about the institutions which operated in this area from 1933 to 1945. The basement of the building contains former Gestapo cells which chill the visitor when their meaning is validated in combination with documents and photographic evidence of the Jewish Holocaust. The museum shop contains documentary texts but, significantly, no souvenirs or catering is available. Similarly chilling and interpreted in a similar manner, the house of the Wannsee Conference, located in respectable suburban Berlin was where the 'Final

Solution' was formalized into a strategic action plan. It is difficult to find, being about 30 minutes walk from the nearest station, but has about 170,000 visitors per annum, half German and half Jewish from around the world. The house is owned by the Senate of the City of Berlin and the exhibition is run by two Jewish trusts. There is no retailing, the emphasis being upon the promotion of a reverential silence and upon the reading of large display boards accompanied by many disturbing photographs of the implementation of the plan which emanated from this building in 1942. Even more difficult to find, the Gedenkstätte Plötzensee memorial is situated on an industrial estate at the place where those party to the attempt to assassinate Hitler were interrogated and executed. Information is available to those who managed to find their way to this memorial which was not marked clearly on the tourist maps widely available. Apart from the memorial itself, the exhibits comprise the five hooks used to hang the conspirators, an event filmed and later shown in the Reichstag. A small information booth provides English translations of the sign boards, but little else.

Located in the former east of the city and taking about two hours to reach from central Berlin, Sachsenhausen was a camp first used for political dissidents (due to its proximity to the capital) and then as a transit camp for Jews during the implementation of the Final Solution. Finally, it returned to its original use after 1945 when it was re-opened to imprison opponents of the Communist regime. The overall feeling of the area is that of a country park in the UK, with many of the visitors obviously participating in a recreational day trip. Much of the interpretation has not been 'revised' since re-unification, and so is a good example of the Honecker regime's approach. Testimony to the defeat of the Nazis by the anti-Fascist forces of Marxism–Leninism is loudly proclaimed from a number of plaques. However, suspicion of the ideological content at this (and, indeed, any other) site must be accompanied by the stark horror of some of the exhibits and photographs. Unlike, say, Auschwitz, there is no lower age limit upon entry and young children can be seen wandering around sites of systematic killings and among images of surgical operations conducted to 'prove' Nazi versions of medical and anthropological sciences. There is a small shop with a limited number of books, but neither souvenirs nor catering are on sale. Also associated with the former 'East', the area around the former Checkpoint

Charlie, symbolic fulcrum of the Cold War, is currently being redeveloped for business use. The gatehouse itself still stands, but access to it is difficult and renders little for the visitor to see. However, nearby, the Museum at Checkpoint Charlie is run by a charitable trust which is driven by an ethos of non-violent social change in the struggle for civil rights. It contains several demonstrations of means of escape across the wall and houses a number of interpretative exhibits highlighting other struggles for human rights, giving particular prominence to Gandhi, Martin Luther King, the events at Tiananmen Square, etc. Admission is charged and there is a shop containing a range of souvenirs.

The largely low-key, and reflective exhibitions in Berlin contrast sharply with that which has been itemized above in respect of the Pacific War. Nevertheless, these represent the past as, somehow, separated from the present – an untrustworthy and vicious Nazi government (not to mention that of East Germany) is contrasted with an enlightened present in which information about these events is freely made available as both admonition and as historical source. Aside from the Museum at Checkpoint Charlie and the relics of the former East, there is little attempt to interpret events within a wider context of time or space – whether accurate or not. Thus, the past is disconnected from the present and the potential guilt of an older generation is masked as if an aberration from another place. The significance of the Final Solution is apparent at Wannsee, but not the implications for those who put it into practice, and those who colluded – few could argue that the industrial scale of death being planned could not have been apparent to those who were responsible for its administration, or those who would have noticed disappearances or train movements. Sites possess a veneer of objectivity, but suffer from a lack of analysis – almost the opposite of the problem encountered by the Smithsonian.

Sites in the SE of England tend to be associated with wartime technology, secrecy and the effects upon urban populations. The Imperial War Museum site in Lambeth is a publicly-owned museum and re-opened to controversy over its charging policy. It presents and interprets artefacts from home and abroad associated with wars in which Britain has been involved during the twentieth century. Not surprisingly, many exhibits are of fighting machines, uniforms and weapons. However, recent developments have included the 'Trench

23   *Museum at Checkpoint Charlie, Berlin*

24   *Memorial to civil rights protestors at Birmingham, Alabama*

Experience', which commodifies the life, sights, sounds and smells of life in the trenches during the First World War, and the 'Blitz Experience' which includes the replication of an air raid while sitting in an Anderson shelter, and a viewing of the consequent destruction to the City of London upon departure. These 'experiences' complement the huge range of artefacts, whether military or social in significance, which interpret wars of the twentieth century in the totality of their campaigns and battles. The museum operates its own shop which has doubled in size recently and which offers both books for the 'serious' scholar and souvenirs for the visitor. A café is franchised to a national catering agency. An outpost of the Imperial War Museum, the Cabinet War Rooms in Great George Street are the 'surviving and most important portion of the underground emergency accommodation' provided for Winston Churchill's Cabinet and advisers during the Second World War. These attempt to overlay the story of the war with an inter-pretation of the events which occurred at this 'real' site of national significance from which strategic decisions emanated between 1939 and 1944. Emphasis is upon minimizing the amount of labelling, the curators opting for an audio tour which takes in both operations rooms where incoming bombers were plotted and personal accommodation provided for those working in these rooms, including Winston Churchill. The tour is designed so that exit is effected through the museum shop offering similar products to Lambeth Road, but in a smaller range. A further outpost, Duxford Airfield, Cambridgeshire, is predominantly a museum of wartime aviation, but also houses a collection of ground-based military vehicles including tanks and field guns. Various activities are possible, including a flight in a biplane, and open days are held throughout the year. A large shed holds a number of vehicles displayed in terrain associated with their purpose, including trenches, desert warfare and the capture of Berlin. Once again, income generation is to the fore with cafés and a large shop offering a range of possible purchases consistent with a day out in the countryside. A museum of the US Airforce, to contain a B-52 bomber, is due to open on this site.

In contrast, the commercial facility entitled Winston Churchill's Britain at War Experience can be seen clearly from Tower Bridge station and is prominently visible in busy Tooley Street. It advertises its ability to relate what it was like during the Second World War and to relive 'the horror of the Blitz'. In its main marketing brochure, it suggests, 'Britain is at War . . . and YOU can be in the midst of it. Come back with us on an unforgettable journey back in time to wartime London and the blitz . . . its [sic] the experience of a lifetime' (Britain at War Experience, no date). The entrance area replicates a 1930s Underground station and, via a lift, takes visitors to a lower floor where the experience of sheltering underground and of street life during the Second World War is replicated using a combination of real artefacts and reconstructed models. The culmination of the visit, which is essentially a procession through the exhibits, is a visit to a bombed-out street, complete with lighting and sound effects. Thereafter, exit is via the shop which offers a range of souvenirs aimed at visitors to London and, especially, schoolchildren. The brochure sets out its dual-marketing stalls clearly in its assertion that, 'Britain at War is more than just a tourist attraction . . . its [sic] a unique trip down memory lane for those who lived through these bitter-sweet days and is an educational must for all those too young to remember' (Britain at War Experience, no date). As if to reinforce the message aimed at the National History Curriculum, the brochure comes complete with a personal

25   Scene from Imperial War Museum, Duxford

endorsement from Dame Vera Lynn who 'thought . . . [she] . . . was back in the war' and who believes that 'all children should visit this nostalgic and moving experience'.

Two sites outside London also merit some analysis. First, Bletchley Park in Milton Keynes is the site of Britain's main codebreaking activities during the Second World War and has been opened to the public by a voluntary body, the Bletchley Park Trust, which markets it as 'Britain's Best Kept Secret'. As the existence of Bletchley Park (location of Robert Harris' novel *Enigma*) only became apparent in recent years, it offers a somewhat different view of the war – mainly from the perspective of the 1,200 men and women who worked at the site when it was the Government Code and Cipher School, whether as cryptologists or in other roles, e.g. in the construction of the world's first electronic valve computer. Principally the trustees aim to develop the site into a major attraction, asserting, as they do, that it 'change[d] the course of world history' (Bletchley Park Trust, 1995a) and that it was the home to 'wartime codebreaking that ended W.W.II two years early and saved many hundreds of thousands of lives' (Bletchley Park Trust, 1995b). In particular, the Trust wishes to 'encourage any other museum's development on the site, particularly of a high-tech nature' (Bletchley Park Trust, 1995b). In essence, this is a museum of tech-nological achievement in saving lives, although objective evidence for the assertions is not provided, which contrasts sharply with the sites and focus upon death and destruction evident in other locations featured in this book. Its clandestine function and its association with a celebrated book, together with the apparent reluctance of the British government to inform its citizens of its existence until the 1970s, qualifies it for an interest in dark tourism. Perhaps of similar tenor in its life-saving orientation and secrecy (it was a state secret until 1988) but on an altogether more significant and gorier scale, Hellfire Corner, in the underground tunnels of Dover Castle, was a military command centre during the Dunkirk evacuation and an underground hospital, mainly for pilots shot down in and around the English Channel. Owned by the English Heritage agency, it adds further to the already popular Dover Castle towering above the celebrated White Cliffs by telling the 'Secret History' of the underground tunnels using sound, sight and smell to recreate the experience (Coad, no date).

To compare and contrast the presentation of war to visitors in Berlin and London would, ultimately, be facile. Such an analysis would point to the differences between victors and vanquished and between market-based and former socialist political ideologies in representing the conflict. More useful, and more challenging, is a consideration of what these sites have in common, particularly where this points to issues for development of further interpretations and opportunities in other cities, such as Belfast (McCafferty, 1995) or Dubrovnik (Desin, 1995).

Drawing together such a wide range of sites in the public, commercial and voluntary sectors into one conceptual framework of tourism supply requires consideration of the common denominators which were present in both élite and 'popular' attractions associated with cataclysmic events. In particular, it is important to differentiate between the dungeons, torture chambers and death sites of earlier European history and representations of the recent past. This analysis is based upon the idea that news and entertainment media, most especially the development of photography and, thereafter of mass communications, has changed the relationship between people and world events. Thus, an event represented as 'dark tourism' is likely to have taken place in the last hundred years and been brought to the public via modern mass media. The scale and scope of the tourism product are likely to be driven by the media.

Commonly, the sites, personalities and actions represented are seen as being beyond criticism, for example, Churchill or the actions of those wishing to escape from the former East Germany. This concept of a sacred cow can be extended to include the techniques of interpretation themselves in some cases, such as at concentration camps. It is usual for events and actions to be portrayed within an 'educative' context, often with an admonitory tone and this can include some direct extrapolation to the present, e.g. ethnic cleansing in the former Yugoslavia is often equated with the actions of Nazi leaders. Sometimes interpretation conforms to the needs of a National History Curriculum, such as the Jewish Holocaust in Germany or social life in the Second World War in Britain.

Although there do not appear to be any unifying geographical factors, such as urban or rural, in dark tourism, it is most likely that only large cities will have a sufficient tourism demand base to allow this particular niche market to be developed. However, this may depend upon the scale of tragedy involved, for example, Auschwitz is located in a small town. Although there may be differences between real artefacts and documents, on the one hand, and commodified experiences, on the other, as well as between actual sites and museums of objects, in practice, these may be of less significance than the way in which the 'story' is told. This may be most important in those facilities which aim predominantly at an education market and where the need to relate the events at a particular site can be constricting compared to the 'freedom' to relate a series of diverse events using film and objects to represent an (apparently) coherent and consistent story. Dark tourism is likely to involve some element of storytelling, although the ideological and political elements of the message are likely to dominate, even at the expense of sensitivity to relatives and victims – e.g. how do victims and families of victims feel about the Checkpoint Charlie museum, Sachsenhausen or the Britain at War Experience? Similarly, although not necessarily simultaneously, sourcing and merchandising of appropriate products for sale at sites and museums are likely to be a complex affair reflecting and reconciling both dominant ethical and cultural values in the host community as well as commercial considerations of marketability and profitability.

The reduction of the distances between the primacy of objects and commodified 'experiences', between story and history, between representation and reality, points to an essentially post-modern phenomenon, especially when taken in combination with the promotion of a consumer culture. In these respects, London may be a more 'mature' tourism product, having progressed towards a post-modern tourism of war. However, particularly in the ways in which the Berlin Wall is being represented to tourists, there are signs that moves are being made away from primary sources and evidence as a basis for interpretation towards commodified experiences, possibly away from the site of the Wall itself. The Federal Government of Germany has been quick to recognize the tourist potential of the Cold War and interest in objects from that period. Notably, in Hotensleben (some 185 km from Berlin) DM 135k has been spent on the repair and rebuilding of the Wall, complete with guard towers and spotlights (*Financial Times*, 16 March 1995). After initial dismantling, some 330 metres will be reconstructed for the purposes of a visitor centre.

26   *Section of the Berlin Wall outside the Imperial War Museum, London*

It is convenient to see Berlin and London as two points on a continuum of this type of tourism development. Future developments beyond those which are evident in London may be seen in the US Holocaust Memorial Museum in Washington, DC, a city which has no direct connection with that event or the Black Museum in St Augustine, Florida containing artefacts from tragedies around the world (but none from Florida). Whatever their merits, these museums exploit awareness of, and interest in, the events which they commemorate, together with their proximity to other tourism venues of major international significance as a recipe for success.

War in Belgium and France

Opportunities for visits to First and Second World War battle sites in France and Belgium from Britain have grown considerably as possibilities for cheap travel have emerged in the last fifteen years. Companies such as Holt's Battlefield Tours now offer tailored packages for those interested in visiting these sites, using a coach service from London. In addition, school trips and the itineraries of more general tours to Belgium and France take in significant sites connected to the First and Second World Wars. Although not wholly merchandised in this way, the activities of tour companies and the promotional efforts of local tourism agencies have enabled complete packages to be bought as a commodity or for visitors to assemble their own itineraries based upon clearly marked and signed routes. In this section, two types of this kind of product are examined, a battlefield tour of First World War sites and self-drive routes packaged by local tourism agencies in Normandy, which lead to the main sites of the D-Day landings and the Battle of Normandy.

Holt's Tours have for many years operated a three-day tour of First World War sites from their base in Sandwich, Kent. Under the title 'It's a Long Way to Tipperary', the tour takes in the British Expeditionary Force route to Ypres and a number of Commonwealth War Graves Commission cemeteries (including Poperinghe, Brandhoek) as well as the playing of the 'Last Post' at the Menin Gate Memorial in Ypres, for which traffic is halted each evening. A German cemetery is also

27   *British Memorial to the Battle of the Somme, Thiépval, France*

visited at Langemarck as well as Canadian sites, including the memorial and tunnels at Vimy Ridge, a significant Allied victory. The tour culminates at the Somme battlefield and associated towns and sights, including the Memorial to the missing at Thiépval. The tours can accommodate the possibility of visiting the graves of relatives for those on the coach. The services of a guide and the use of audio and visual aids while the coach is travelling add to the overall package. On each tour the group collectively lays a wreath at one of the War graves. A main focus is to identify 'interesting' graves, such as those of holders of the Victoria Cross or of especially young casualties.

The tour depends heavily upon the sites of the Commonwealth War Graves Commission (CWGC), a governmental agency, which was set up (as the Imperial War Graves Commission) to commemorate the dead of the First World War and has gone on to take responsibility for British military casualties throughout the world (Longworth, 1985). As the keeper of records of deaths, each CWGC site contains names of all of those contained or commemorated at the cemetery. Clearly, such sites are associated with remembrance and do not possess any forms of interpretation or commerciality – indeed, some are, literally, in corners of foreign fields in Belgium and Northern France surrounded by local agriculture. Equally important is the town of Ypres in Flanders, where a number of local sites are used to interpret the activities of the early parts of the war, especially from local vantage points of height (of which there are few). Most poignant is the Menin Gate, inscribed with the names of Allied troops who died in the Ypres Salient and who have no known graves. As the local guidebook says, 'This is no mute memorial, standing unnoticed for most of the year. It straddles one of the busiest roads in town, a constant reminder of sacrifice. Once a day it resounds with a living tribute from the people of Ypres; at 8pm buglers of the Ypres Fire Brigade sound the Last Post' (Evans, 1992).

Of critical importance to the Holt's Tour, and to the tourist product offered in relation to the First World War, is the entire landscape on offer – a key part of the strategic and operational actuality of the war and its events as they unfolded in Belgium and Northern France. The cemeteries and monuments of Verdun, the Somme and the sites of other major battles are located on relatively high ground, which offers the visitor an overview of the fields of battle and, although these quickly returned to (predominantly) agricultural use after the war, visitors are encouraged to envisage the scene and the tactical problems from within the landscape itself – thereby offering the countryside as a perpetual and living museum of the war. This possibility is reinforced by the frequently repeated fact that military ordnance continues to be ploughed up in the fields by local farmers.

The careful, but relatively informal, use of landscape to evoke memory, remembrance and quasi-representation offered by the organized battlefield tour is taken a step further in Normandy where a significant proportion of the tourism product is devoted to those visiting the beaches and battlefields associated with the D-Day campaign. This is called the 'Open-Air Museum of the Battle of Normandy' by tourist authorities (Gallimard, no date). Essentially, a series of guided itineraries with supporting guidebooks and maps enables the visitor to pursue various elements of the battle via colour-coded signposts and routes among the beaches, countryside, and the detritus of the decisive campaign of the Second World War in Europe. It is surely no coincidence that these itineraries enable the visitor to reach almost all of the

Normandy area. There are a total of eight routes, namely *Overlord* – *L'Assaut*; *D.Day* – *Le Choc*; *Objectif* – *Un Port*; *L'Affrontement Cobra* – *La Percée*; *La Contre* – *Attaque*; *L'Encerclement*; *Le Dénouement*. Each of these contains a range of sites from formal museums, such as *Le Mémorial* – *Un Musée pour la Paix* in Caen (which extends its remit beyond the campaign itself into conflict in the twentieth century and includes, strangely, Pol Pot's writing desk from his days at the Sorbonne) or the *Musée Mémorial de la Bataille de Normandie* in Bayeux or the *Musée de la Libération* in Cherbourg, to actual sites of battles (e.g. Utah, Juno, Sword, Omaha and Gold Beaches – some more 'unspoilt' than others), to the remains of Hitler's defences (known as the Atlantic Wall) which are now preserved as monuments along parts of the coast (e.g. *Batterie de Longues*) or have been 'converted' into museums where they are sufficiently large and close enough to other touristic opportunities (e.g. the *Musée du Mur de l'Atlantique* in a suburb of Ouistreham). Similarly, Allied hardware left to rot has presented opportunities for the entrepreneur at Port-en Bessin (*Musée des Épaves Sous-marines du Débarquement*) and at many other sites, such as at Arromanches. Finally, the war graves and cemeteries of the American, British, French, Canadian, Polish and German armies, mostly close to the beaches mentioned above where the most popular areas for visitation are, receive huge numbers of casual, informal and organized visits every year. Of course, every city, town and village has a memorial and, often a street name, to commemorate the Liberation and some offer visitors a further tale to detain them a little longer than might otherwise be the case.

The countrysides of Belgium and Northern France (representing the First World War) and Normandy (representing the Second) show some significant differences from the other sites examined in this chapter for several key reasons. First, the tourist offering is an entire landscape which represents an element of a conflict that covered, in some cases, years. Thus, the scope of what is on offer differs significantly from, say, Pearl Harbor, where a single incident at a contained geographical point is the issue to be considered. This appears to offer the travel agent and tourism planner a number of opportunities to disperse the tourism (and, undoubtedly, its benefits) across a far wider area where a much larger range of small businesses may benefit from visitor spending. It also

28   *Sign on Tourist Trail, Normandy, France*

enables the 'dark' element of the tourism to be located within a wider
tourist product (e.g. the Bayeux Tapestry in Normandy). The London
destroyed in the Blitz no longer exists – it is not a landscape to be visited
like the Somme or Omaha Beach – and is available only as a
representation in a tourist experience constructed within a museum.
Second, it is clear that the historical events portrayed in these
landscapes, while continuing to be seen as horrific (witness the film
Saving Private Ryan), are also seen to have been resolved by many of
those who visit, whether to remember the dead or to interpret historical
events. Politically, the significance of Flanders or the Normandy Beaches
has been interpreted as the creation of a new world order (with the
caveat offered at the *Musée pour la Paix*) which has led to a rational
reconfiguration of Western Europe and its economies. This
rationalization is far less clear in the case of the war between the USA
and Japan or even, until very recently, in Berlin. Finally, with specific
reference to Normandy, there is an evident tourism strategy at play
whereby the most popular sites, which are coastal, are used to
encourage the visitor to travel further into parts of the region which
receive fewer visitors but which can be stimulated by a relatively small

29   *First house liberated by Allied troops, Normandy, France*

increase in expenditure. Moreover, the strategy involves appearing to concede the power to decide upon movements to the car-borne visitor, thereby introducing an element of freedom and interpretation which is currently absent elsewhere in dark tourism.

CHAPTER EIGHT

North Cyprus: Disappointing
Performance with 'Dark' Edges

A recent review of competitive strategies in the context of Northern Cyprus provided a useful overview of tourism to the Turkish Republic of Northern Cyprus (TRNC) (Altinay and Biçak, 1997). Yet this is an island state which faces unique problems in terms of tourism development that merits further analysis. Indeed, aspects of the separation of this nation allude to a 'darker' period of the island's history which remains unresolved and of international concern.

The Turkish Republic of Northern Cyprus – context and perspective

The island of Cyprus and the uneasy accord between Greek and Turkish Cypriots remain 'unacceptable' for many organizations and countries (most notably the UN, the EU and the governments of Turkey, Greece, the USA and the UK). Invariably, tragic cases are promoted on both sides, from the case of the 110–220,000 Cypriot Greek refugees who were forced to leave their homes and lives in the north, following the intervention of the Turkish military in 1974, to the 50,000 Turkish refugees moved to the north of the island. It should be noted that the Turkish refugees do not wish to return and do not feel deprived of their human rights. Yet the economic development of the north since 1974 has been seriously affected by the denunciation of the development of the TRNC by the UN Security Council and the subsequent economic boycotts by the EU and other powers. Indeed, such exclusive sanctions against the TRNC have resulted in greater economic integration with Turkey and a greater reluctance to consider any steps towards union with the south.

The exact number of refugees has been the subject of some dispute. Cypriot Greek figures quote a total figure of in excess of 220,000 whilst the British Parliamentary Group, the Friends of Northern Cyprus, quote figures of closer to 105,000. More recent commentators place the figure at closer to 140–160,000 (see, for example, Dodd, 1995). There remains much bitterness and a deep sense of injustice on both sides. Indeed, the very existence of the Turkish Republic of Northern Cyprus has remained internationally unrecognized by other sovereign powers and the related division of Cyprus remains a major impediment in relation to Turkey's proposed entry to the EU (*The Economist*, 1997, 1998a).

Yet peace reigns on either side of the UN policed divide; there are no deaths, no terrorism and the effects of the division are perhaps more widely felt in the international arena of world politics, rather than at a local level. For example, the Greek veto on Turkey's entry to the EU is predicated upon a solution to the 'Cyprus problem' and continually attracts international attention (*The Economist*, 1998a, 1998b).

Unrecognized as a sovereign state, the TRNC remains substantially supported by direct subsidy and preferential export terms from Turkey. Indeed, the cause of the dismal performance of tourism to the island is directly associated with this political situation rather than the 'competitive' factors identified by some tourism academics (Altinay and Biçak, 1997). In tourism terms, more longitudinal comparison of statistics illustrate the dismal performance of the north in comparison with its southern neighbour. Tourist arrivals from 1986–96 (see Table 8.1) clearly indicate the low levels of international tourism and the continued significance of air transport to the region.

The erratic performance should not detract attention from what is essentially a pitifully small number of incoming visitors. At the same time, world tourism and tourism to the south of the island (the Republic of Cyprus) has grown at an unprecedented rate (WTO, 1997; Witt, 1991).

Table 8.1   Number of arrivals by mode of travel, 1986–96

Years	Arrivals by sea			Arrivals by air	Total arrivals
	Kyrenia	Famagusta	Total		
1986	15,970	80,447	96,417	90,151	186,568
1987	29,593	92,089	121,682	121,952	243,634
1988	74,102	62,592	136,694	152,885	289,579
1989	112,648	59,689	172,337	170,319	342,656
1990	46,762	118,244	165,006	210,485	375,491
1991	77,538	40,887	118,425	167,824	286,249
1992	86,007	26,253	112,260	233,824	346,084
1993	114,543	26,164	140,707	312,275	452,982
1994	140,993	32,284	173,277	288,138	461,415
1995	157,906	26,829	184,735	335,398	520,133
1996	157,172	24,310	181,482	316,706	498,188

(*Source*: TRNC, 1996)

Further analysis of Table 8.1 reveals even poorer performance if one considers the origins of tourists. It is apparent that Table 8.1 is inflated by the presence of TRNC residents (domestic holiday makers) and Table 8.2 gives a more accurate perspective as well as highlighting the centrality of the Turkish market for this destination.

The problematic nature of air access to this part of the island is reaffirmed by the breakdown of visitor numbers (by origin) detailed in Table 8.3. Seaborne tourists are overwhelmingly Turkish in origin. Air travel restrictions mean access for international tourists is difficult. Indeed, the cost and journey to the TRNC are extended considerably because of the issue of political recognition. Turkey is the sole nation recognizing the sovereignty of the TRNC and this means that currently there are no direct scheduled flights to the TRNC from any nation other than Turkey. Accordingly, all incoming flights must route via Turkey and then use a Turkish carrier to enter via air. This incurs significant cost increases for the consumer, that are directly linked to touchdown

Table 8.2   Number of arrivals by country of usual residence, 1986–96

Years	Turkey	Other countries	Total tourist arrivals	TRNC arrivals	Total arrivals	Total arrivals less TRNC
1986	105,729	25,763	131,492	55,076	186,568	131,492
1987	147,965	36,372	184,337	59,297	243,634	184,337
1988	173,351	56,050	229,401	60,178	289,579	229,401
1989	214,566	59,507	274,073	68,583	342,656	274,073
1990	243,269	57,541	300,810	74,681	375,491	300,810
1991	179,379	40,858	220,237	66,012	286,249	220,237
1992	210,178	57,440	267,618	78,466	346,084	267,618
1993	281,370	77,943	359,313	93,669	452,982	359,313
1994	256,549	95,079	351,628	109,787	461,415	450,437
1995	298,026	87,733	385,759	134,374	520,133	385,759
1996	289,131	75,985	365,116	133,072	498,188	365,116

(*Source*: TRNC, 1996)

expenses in Turkey. This extends journey time, normally by up to three hours, making this one of the most difficult Mediterranean locations to visit.

Transport difficulties offer no such problems for tourists to the southern half of the island where Nicosia International Airport, as the major gateway, has contributed significantly to the tourism performance of the south (Witt, 1991). UN economists on a number of occasions have noted that the opening of this airport to the TRNC would allow the north to prosper significantly from European tourism (as has the south). Yet this would significantly reduce the Greek Cypriot dominance of the island's economic growth and is unlikely to be conceded unless the issue of 'sovereignty' in a new federal state is resolved.

Other performance indicators for the TRNC, most notably accommodation occupancy (in percentages) in the tourism sector, are indicative of the poor performance of the sector overall (see Table 8.4). As a

Table 8.3 Number of tourists by country of usual residence and percentage of total in 1996

Country of usual residence	No. of tourists	Percentage
Turkey	70,519	48.13
England	26,091	17.80
Germany	17,576	11.98
Austria	1,605	1.09
France	2,412	1.61
Russia	1,006	0.69
Denmark	952	0.65
Finland	471	0.32
Italy	422	0.29
Holland	222	0.16
Switzerland	74	0.05
Belgium	60	0.04
Sweden	43	0.03
Macedonia	8	0.01
Other	5,266	3.60
TRNC	19,869	13.55
Total	146,668	100.00

(Source: TRNC, 1996)

consequence, employment in the sector is similarly low and has sustained poor growth over recent years (see Table 8.5).

The travel and tourism sector provides one in every nine jobs world-wide (WTTC, 1995). The dismal level of employment generation in tourism in the TRNC is indicative of the wider political and economic difficulties this state is experiencing. Finally, the net income from tourism shows equally disappointing results (see Table 8.6).

Image and market development in the TRNC have been consistent in branding this part of the island as Northern Cyprus (see, for example,

Table 8.4 Room occupancy rates in tourist accommodation by years (%)

Years	Occupancy rates (%)
1986	21.5
1987	46.3
1988	45.8
1989	41.2
1990	37.6
1991	22.6
1992	31.6
1993	36.8
1994	37.3
1995	37.5
1996	32.5

(*Source*: TRNC, 1996)

Table 8.6 Net tourism income by years

Year	Net tourism income (million US$)
1986	57.9
1987	103.5
1988	118.0
1989	154.9
1990	224.8
1991	153.6
1992	175.1
1993	224.6
1994	172.9
1995	218.9
1996	180.3

(*Source:* TRNC, 1996)

Table 8.5 Number of employees in tourist establishments, 1994–6

Type of establishments	1994		1995		1996	
	No. of establishments	No. of employees	No. of establishments	No. of employees	No. of establishments	No. of employees
Hotels, hotel-apts. and others	78	2,276	78	2,177	81	2,457
Guest-houses	15	48	15	50	18	62
Restaurants	470	1,880	605	1,946	558	2,146
Travel agencies	155	375	164	408	161	410
Total	718	4,579	862	4,581	818	5,075

(*Source:* TRNC, 1996)

in North Cyprus, 1997, and Yayinlari and North Cyprus Museum Friends, 1995). The brand 'Northern Cyprus' like the 'official' title TRNC are both of little use in postal terms. Given the pariah status of this nation, all mail is routed through Turkey with the telling but necessary postal address: 'Mersin – IO, Turkey' (North Cyprus, 1997).

Furthermore, tourism publications, promotion materials and attraction descriptions often offer unusual political inserts and references to the military intervention that are clearly ideological in their references to the period of partition and conflict. The 1997 brochure on North Cyprus includes some two pages of historical commentary, which incorporates a highly detailed, overtly political commentary on the 1974 division and more recent events. It is detailed below:

> As regards the [sic] legality of the intervention of Turkey, interesting is the decision of the High Court of Athens (N.2658/79) of March 21st 1979:

> The Intervention of Turkey in Cyprus as one of the Guarantor Power within the Framework of Zurich and London agreements is legal. Actually the Greek officers against whom the court cases have been brought, are responsible for the intervention. Turkey was among the Guarantors of the Republic of Cyprus. General Joannides and his 102 colleagues endangered the integrity of the Republic of Cyprus and created the climate for the intervention . . .

> **1974–1995**
> In recent history . . . The island today enjoys a great internal tranquillity even if the economic development of Northern Cyprus is slow, hampered as it is by the embargo enforced by Greece and the Greek Cypriots on this part of the Island.

> (North Cyprus, 1997, p. 5)

The inclusion of such information in marketing and promotional materials reflects the distrust and darker elements of this island's tourism product.

A number of attractions which are referred to in tourism guides and publications, notably, the Museum of the National Dispute, and the

Museum of the Atrocity, offer clearly ideological interpretations of the dispute and events since 1974. Furthermore, border points in the Demilitarized Zone (DMZ) have themselves become attractions. Indeed, the DMZ exerts a 'dark' fascination for many visitors on both the southern and northern sides of the island. This DMZ (known in the TRNC as the 'Forbidden Zone') which bisects the island landscape and the capital of Nicosia (Lefkosa) has unintentionally become a tourist destination. It is one of the last clear national military borders left in the post-Cold War environment (North and South Korea offering another). The haunting empty buildings and roads long unused, with vegetation emerging, are reminiscent of a film set or images of empty cities in more tragic contexts.

Interestingly, interpretation of the border is carried out on both the Turkish Cypriot and Greek Cypriot sides, where the victims of the various murderous and violent acts are exhibited in photographic form for visitors to view. What is on offer on either side of this border is a twin reflection of a shared past: in a most literal form the interpretative display offers a 'mirror' image of a dark past on either side.

The reflection is echoed in language regarding the dispute in many aspects of this border interpretation. On the Greek Cypriot side the Turkish intervention is referred to as 'the 1974 invasion' while on the TRNC side the same event is referred to as a 'peace operation'. The events of 20 July 1974 remain a topic of emotive, opposing language and history (Matthews, 1987).

On the world political stage, the Cyprus 'issue' may be considered as something of a minor element that works against Turkey's EU membership and frustrates politicians looking for a negotiated settlement. In conflict terms, few now are killed and peace almost reigns. Yet the animosity between the Greek and Turkish sides remains and the 'unacceptable' movement of displaced persons remains a huge stumbling block to any future reconciliation (*The Economist*, 1998b).

The deep sense of injustice felt on both sides began in 1963–4 when Greek Cypriots indicated clearly that the Cypriot Turks were a minority and tried to coerce them into this view. The policy of *enosis* sought to embrace Cyprus with the Hellenic (Greek) world via an identification with a shared classical past. Cypriot Turks, a sizeable minority population, were enraged by UN recognition of the Cypriot Greek government as the legitimate government of Cyprus. On the Greek Cypriot side, the

30   *Border point, Turkish Republic of Northern Cyprus*

Cyprus problem really only began in 1974 with the Turkish invasion of approximately one-third of the Island. The condemnation by the Greek Cypriots of the West for allowing this to occur was forceful. Consequently, claims for sovereignty and legality made by the TRNC have long remained unacceptable to Greece and the Greek Cypriots (Republic of Cyprus). Furthermore, the doctrine of both *enosis* and the *megali* ideal embraces the concept that both historically and culturally Cyprus is a Greek island (Dodd, 1995). Such powerful national sentiment is very strong and reflected in aspects of the tourism product. Maps and tourist guides originating in the Republic of Cyprus are damning and incorrect in their labelling of the north as 'inaccessible' to visitors and under 'Turkish occupation' (Akis and Warner, 1994). This disguises the truth of the region, which though problematic to reach, does offer a range of facilities, landscape and attractions.

Northern Cyprus (TRNC) for some academics (see Lockhart, 1994) offers a laboratory for the observations of long-term effects of military intervention and diplomatic isolation on tourist development. Indeed, the international 'pariah' status of the TRNC has of course impacted on marketing and promotion. The non-recognition of the TRNC by tour

31   *Denktash image, City Square, Lefkosa, Turkish Republic of*
     Northern Cyprus

operators is a direct consequence, since wholesale marketing of 'North Cyprus' as a destination cannot be undertaken for fear of antagonizing the trading relationship with southern Cyprus and Greece (Lockhart, 1994). These two popular destinations for European tourists simply cannot be antagonized by any of the major tour operators who wish to offer comprehensive Mediterranean coverage. This has of course resulted in low levels of accommodation demand, pitiful occupancy and a consequently low economic impact by tourism on the TRNC (TRNC, 1996; Biçak and Altinary, 1996). It may be argued that this has limited the negative environmental impact of tourism and accordingly this feature could be used to positively 'sell' the north. Notably, this theme is evident in some branding; see, for example, 'North Cyprus – A Sanctuary of Unspoilt Beauty' (Noble Caledonian Limited, 1998). This company attempts to reverse the negative aspects of undevelopment and positively use this to sell the destination. The quote below is taken from a newspaper advertisement:

> You will not find Northern Cyprus in the large tour operator's brochures and consequently the number of visitors is relatively small and the tourism development limited.
>
> For some the lack of development is a minus, whilst for others it will be the strongest reason for travelling there. In many ways the atmosphere is similar to that you would have experienced in Mediterranean resorts some 30 to 40 years ago before the advent of the package tour. If, like us, you are attracted by places which still have a natural charm, warm and friendly inhabitants, quiet beaches and ancient sites where you may be the only visitor, then Northern Cyprus might be the ideal place for you. (Sunday Review, *Independent on Sunday*, 21 June 1998, p. 50)

Yet the brochure text and the imagery of 'North Cyprus – A Corner of the Earth touched by Heaven' (City Plan of Lefkosa, 1997) fail to mention the environmental impact of over 30,000 Turkish military personnel, whose significant presence is evident throughout rural and urban areas. Military areas are designated in Kyrenia, Varosha, and a number of camps may be found on the Mesaoria Plain and in areas along the Demilitarized Zone. Indeed, the deterioration of buildings in these military/security zones is considerable, with the dense undergrowth harbouring a variety of problematic vermin (Lockhart, 1994). The DMZ, which straddles the island like a latter-day Berlin Wall, encases houses, hotels, roads, traffic signals, cars and gardens that all remain deserted. On the TRNC side, its title 'the Forbidden Zone', does little to deter the intrigued tourists attracted to this unusual phenomena. Like the Texas School Book Depository building in Dallas, this DMZ offers a picture of Cyprus frozen in time, that motivates a curious fascination among tourists peering into this decaying central divide. Potentially, for both sides, a significant tourist attraction remains undeveloped, a silent sentinel guarding against reunification and reconciliation. Yet its presence as a tourist 'draw' remains officially ignored and discouraged by the authorities.

More overtly, in tourism terms, the conflict features in a commodified form in the tourist brochures for TRNC locations such as Nicosia. The major city tourist brochure notes the following: 'Places worth a visit: Barbarian Museum, National Dispute Museum (City Plan of Lefkosa, 1997, p. 1). Both of these museums offer directed interpretation and a stylized version of the 1974 dispute. Both museums feature gratuitous photography of atrocities committed against the Turkish side, while in the Republic of Cyprus similar displays of Turkish atrocities perpetrated against the Greek Cypriots feature at the border point (Ledra Gate). Thus aspects of the dispute are commodified as part of the tourist experience with the overt support of the authorities. Indeed, such commodification extends to mapping and the lack of the official recognition of the TRNC regime, and is reflected directly in the tourist maps of the Republic of Cyprus, which describe the TRNC as simply 'inaccessible to visitors' (Akis and Warner, 1994) while conversely detailing a border crossing point.

The conflict within the island both negates tourism flows in the north and inflates official tourism statistics. The UN troops in the DMZ and elsewhere have been referred to by the TRNC President, Rauf Denktash, as 'permanent tourists'. Simply put, it is his quoted belief that their role as consumers outweighs their value as peacekeepers (op. cit., p. 387). Tourism statistics to the TRNC are also influenced directly by the undeveloped infrastructure and problematic access on the TRNC side. Tourist maps feature both Greek Cypriot and Turkish city names yet go on to describe only 37 per cent of the land, cities and selective elements of history. The division is reflected geographically and metaphorically (see, for example, North Cyprus, 1997). The country (TRNC) is described as if the south does not exist with references to language, currency, cities and population. Such selective attention is also evident in the tourism promotion brochures of the Republic of Cyprus (in, for example, *Welcome to Cyprus*, 1997) wherein a similar level of selective interpretation is evident.

In TRNC visitor numbers, the dominance of Turkish visitors followed the Turkish military intervention of 1974. Much of the motivation for

32   *Forbidden Zone (Demilitarized Zone), Turkish Republic of*
Northern Cyprus

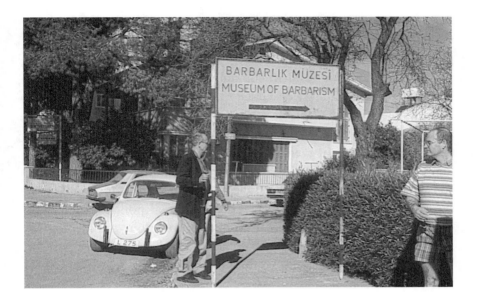

33   Museum of Barbarism, Turkish Republic of Northern Cyprus

visitation was by families and friends visiting military personnel. Turkish residents could now visit a country that was freely accessible to them and offered considerable potential for black market/'suitcase' trading (Akis and Warner, 1994). Yet the decline in the Turkish economy, problems with currency, and a general economic downturn since 1994, have significantly impacted on the downward trend in tourism to the TRNC.

The reality for the Republic of Cyprus has been well charted (see Witt, 1991; Andronicou, 1979). The partition of 1974, while significantly damaging infrastructure and resulting in a considerable loss in bed accommodation, helped catalyse the development of new bed stock and led to significant growth in tourism facilities in tourist areas in the south. The 1980s saw significant growth in tourism terms with tourism making a very significant contribution to the economy, even though the environmental impact has been at times problematic (Witt, 1991). Yet, as a destination, the popularity of the Republic of Cyprus is only occasionally shattered, and then the 2 million international visitors per year become uneasy. Simply put, promoting Cyprus will be difficult if alarming news headlines report the incidents of inter-communal violence. Cyprus is a forcibly divided island on which some 30,000 Turkish troops are stationed. Several people have died in outbreaks of inter-communal violence, most particularly in the summer of 1997 (Drake, 1997, p. 25 [1]). Cyprus is one of the most densely militarized countries in the world with a deeply divided resident community. These two people mistrust each other greatly, almost no Greek Cypriot speaks a word of Turkish and very few Turkish Cypriots speak any Greek. Tourism interpretation and promotional material have been effectively used to promote a problematic history of events since 1974. This interpretation reflects a 'dark' point of mutual distrust, aggression and violence that has consequently developed an unofficially recognized visitor attraction in the DMZ partition that so well reflects the real politics of Cyprus. Mutual mistrust, selective attention in interpretation, and ideological sentiment evident in publications, do not fail to disguise a dark past for both sides in a seemingly intractable conflict.

CHAPTER NINE

Dislocation: The US Holocaust Memorial Museum

In the post-modern condition, reality is a matter for debate. As far as tourism is concerned, the emergence of simulations, replications and virtual experiences as part of the tourism product has been a critical factor in the development of dark tourism. For example, the US Holocaust Memorial Museum in Washington, DC, a Federally chartered institution, has received visitation levels of in excess of 2 million per annum since its opening in April 1993. Built with $168 million in private

34   US Holocaust Memorial Museum, Washington, DC

funds, it is the first major cultural institution to open in Washington in the last ten years. Notwithstanding the gravity of its subject matter, neither the site of the museum (in downtown Washington) nor many of the displays (some of which are replicas) have an 'authentic' connection with the Jewish Holocaust. Moreover, a feature of the experience of the museum for the user is the acceptance of the identity of a Jewish citizen of Hitler's Germany. This identity is presented on a card gained upon entry which can be updated at various stages in the visitor 'progress' through the museum – intimating whether 'you' have been arrested, imprisoned, transported to a concentration camp, gassed, etc. Some commentators have drawn attention to the irony of 'discarded' identities in litter bins at exit points and on the street outside the museum. Nevertheless, the museum in total presents a powerful experience which its market research indicates evokes a strong and largely favourable response from visitors (Eskenazi, 1994a).

Memory and remembrance are central to this aspect of tourism. As Young notes:

> Remembrance as a vital human activity shapes our links to the past, and the ways we remember define us in the present. As individuals and societies, we need the past to construct and to anchor our identities and to nurture a vision of the future . . . However, we know how slippery and unreliable personal memory can be, always affected by forgetting and denial, repression and trauma, and, more often than not, serving the need to rationalize and to maintain power. But a society's collective memory is no less contingent, no less unstable, its shape by no means permanent and always subject to subtle and not so subtle reconstruction. (1993, p. 9).

If one considers memory and the representation of the past in the context of dark tourism, one can chart an obsession with the past. This expansive historicism of contemporary culture is something which has dominated museums and memorials. Their historicizing, regeneration of urban centres, creation of conservation/museum villages, the protection of landscapes, the boom in retro fashions and waves of nostalgia, and the academic process of quoting and citing, can be said to function as a key paradigm of post-modern culture. The memorial culture is central to the historical past and in the case of the traumatic event such as the Holocaust, Holocaust museums, memorials and monuments are central to post-modern culture. A central element for retention of a museum/ monument as opposed to its replacement with the television/ media image is the centrality and primacy of the object. Museum objects, whether it be a fortification, site of imprisonment, place of death, take on a key role in a culture that is dominated by moving images and fleeting visions in modern technology. Permanency of monuments, ruins, preserved spaces, can serve to attract a public dissatisfied with constant simulation and media culture of the modern age.

The importance of the site and the primacy of the object have a chronological distance in terms of their permanence. As Primo Levi has noted:

> If, at the time of liberation, we had been asked: 'What would you like to do with these infected barracks, these wire fences, these rows of toilets, these ovens, these gallows?', I think that most of us would have answered: 'Get rid of everything, raze it to the ground along with Nazism and everything German'. We would have said this (and many have by tearing down the barbed wire, and by setting fire to the barracks), and we would have been wrong. These are not mistakes to efface. With the passing of years and decades, their remains do not lose any of their significance as a Warning Monument; rather, they gain in meaning. (1986 p. 185)

Dark tourism is consistent with accounts of post-modernity. The starting point for the authors in conducting research into aspects of heritage and atrocity was that some common threads could be drawn between sites and events of the last century which had either been the locations of death and disaster, or where such events are interpreted 'off-site' for visitors (e.g. the US Holocaust Memorial Museum in Washington, DC). In constructing a vocabulary for these sites and locations, it became clear that the use of the term 'tourist attraction' represented both a judgement about the motives and rationales for making the site available to the public and a commentary about the experiences of visitors.

In this context, the authors have been concerned to establish why some, and not other, events led to certain locations being interpreted and what is involved in the process of moving from death and disaster to 'attraction'. It was of interest to ask why some 'notorious' sites of the twentieth century are offered as heritage attractions, and others are not. For example, the Watergate building in Washington, DC, Hitler's Bunker in Berlin, the Altamont Racetrack in California, and the tunnels of the Securitate in Bucharest, remain undeveloped as attractions.

There are elements of the 'ancient' in dark tourism, for example, in the construction and visitation of sites intended to maintain memory (see, for example, Young, 1993) and there is considerable evidence to suggest that pilgrimage and homage motivations to these monuments have prevailed (Kugelmass, 1994). Visits to those sites which could be termed 'dark' have been analysed by a number of commentators within the framework of modernity (see, for example, Ashworth, 1996). These tend to adopt a perspective of rationality, progress and historicism and stress the 'educative' elements of the offerings. It is not uncommon for there to be a 'visitor centre' located at the site in question and which offers some 'interpretation', via signage and printed material (logocentrism), of the events being considered. Our own work takes this further, discerning limitations of post-modernity in technological approaches to interpretation characterized by iconocentrism and montage, the effect of global communications upon the types of events being offered as tourism products and the strong orientation (in some cases) towards income generation, performativity, commodification and, ultimately, 'entertainment'.

The US Holocaust Memorial Museum, which opened in 1993, has not been short of controversy, and opinion was initially very divided on its purpose, role, and the nature of the message. The question is why does the USA (a country that is 97 per cent non-Jewish) need such a museum? It was not the site of mass execution (Poland), the homeland of the perpetrators (Germany), nor possessed a significant relationship to the victims (Israel). It has been argued that the original proposal for this museum under the then president Jimmy Carter was programmed to appease Jewish supporters angered by the sale of F-15 fighters to Saudi Arabia (for further discussion on the political background to the decision to develop this museum, see Miller, 1990). Its origins, then, were in the Carter administration, wherein the vague idea of a memorial to the Holocaust was originally proposed. Following this a Presidential Commission on the Holocaust was created, incorporating survivors, scholars, researchers and others. Following visits to European sites and concentration camps, a report was produced in September 1979. The report proposed a living memorial museum which would tell the story of the Holocaust. The museum was created by an Act of Congress unanimously approved in 1980 which created a Holocaust Memorial Council of 55, appointed by the President with 5 members of the House of Representatives and 5 members of the US Senate as part of this governing body. The Federal Government agreed to give 1.9 acres of prime land, on condition that all building and equipment costs were funded by private donation. This was done via the highly successful fund-raising programme, 'A Campaign to Remember' (Moore, 1993). Currently, day-to-day operational costs are funded by the Federal Government (approximately $21.2 million in 1993) in order to ensure free access in line with other Washington museums. Targeted direct mail packages specifically designed for certain audiences were one form of fund-raising used. Certain materials were sent to people whose names appeared as predominantly Jewish, whereas a different design package was used for general mailing lists, with the latter stressing the key role of the USA in the Second World War and focusing on the US liberation of Dachau. Just two years from commencement, $10.5 million had been raised by direct mail. Sophisticated narratives focusing on links through religion, culture, and involvement were used in this state-of-the-art campaign. However, such fund-raising activity came in for criticism from the *Washington Post* in 1992 who compared the process of screening surnames to that used by the Nazis to identify Jews.

Interestingly, finance offered by the German government to the development of the museum was also rejected (Polakoff, 1993). An offer was put to the Memorial Council of a 'substantial sum' if the museum incorporated an exhibition on postwar Germany (explaining the 'distance' the new Germany had travelled since the tyranny of the Nazi era). According to the Council's Director of Communications, all foreign government donations were unacceptable as:

This is the American museum built with American funds. We also said Congress mandated the council to portray the events from 1933 through 1945 and therefore we could not in our exhibitions discuss the resurgence of democracy in Germany. (Paiss, quoted in Polakoff, 1993, p. 6)

Further, in this context Paiss (the Holocaust Memorial Council's Director of Communications) noted: 'To my knowledge no other nation asked to change our exhibition in any way' (ibid., p. 6). Yet despite this interchange considerable assistance was offered by the German Government in the sharing of artefacts and materials and the monetary offer was later disputed by the German Embassy in Washington, DC. The German Government's concern with balance and current image as influenced by the museum's effect on visitors seems ill-timed and not thought through. As one representative of the German Chancellery injected:

> We had concerns that a person visiting a museum which reflects only the Nazi times could raise the question of why the United States is in an alliance with such a country . . . we respect the decision that was made to build the museum as it was built. But this doesn't mean that we wouldn't have liked to see it done a little differently. (Atkinson, 1993, p. 3)

35   *Museum of Tolerance at the Simon Wiesenthal Center, Los Angeles*

Interestingly, further criticism of the museum did emerge in the German press with the *Frankfurter Allgemeine* particularly vociferous. Such critique is not new and similar derisive and critical commentaries were offered on the creation of the Museum of Tolerance in Los Angeles (which opened in February 1993) by the German press.

Criticism of the creation of the US Holocaust Memorial Museum from the *Frankfurter Allgemeine* argued that American Jewish organizations use the Holocaust as an ersatz religion to rally support among assimilated Jews. Indeed, the *Frankfurter Allgemeine* reported in a Washington dispatch: 'Half a century after the war's end, is it advisable to lead millions of visitors through a museum that ends in 1945 and thereby may leave the lasting impression, "These are the Germans and this is Germany?"' (Polakoff, 1993, p. 6).

Media and interpretation – the Washington experience

The museum's permanent exhibition, which takes up three floors, contains 5,000 artefacts, including photographs, uniforms, letters, a Polish railcar used to take people to the death camps, and a Danish fishing boat used to transport Jews to safety in Sweden. Through the use of computer terminals, visitors are able to look up old articles from their local papers to see what was being reported about the Holocaust at the time. Theatres are scattered throughout the exhibition. Near the exit, one theatre shows excerpts from more than 200 interviews with witnesses to the Holocaust. Video monitors that display particularly graphic or disturbing material are located behind 'privacy walls' to put them out of sight of children and give visitors a way to avoid viewing them.

Upon leaving the permanent exhibition, visitors are directed to the Hall of Remembrance, a six-sided building where people can reflect on what they have seen. If people want to learn more about the Holocaust, they can visit the museum's Wexner Learning Center which has 24 computer terminals from which people can call up articles about Holocaust-related topics, watch film clips or taped interviews with survivors of the Holocaust, look at maps or photographs, and listen to music.

The concern with replication and simulation is of course central to our treatment and analysis of dark tourism. The concern some may have with the pastiche that such a museum may offer is worthy of further consideration. Does re-creation of objects, utilization of interpretative techniques and experimentation with identity adoption (via the ID card) displace real history behind a façade of education and historical narrative? Not all of the objects are created: authentic cobblestones from the Warsaw Ghetto are used, objects of everyday life (sewing machines, prams, bicycles), as well as a range of other artefacts including inmates' hair, shoes and other remnants from Auschwitz–Birkenau are on display.

Central to the interpretation is the use of newsreels, radio broadcasts, and papers. The reality of the 1930s and 1940s is recreated in the way US citizens were actually informed of the rise of Nazi Germany and the progress of the war. Media once again emerges as central to understanding the interpretation of the events.

Interestingly there is also art in the form of sculpture and painting at various points in the museum. Its presence seems out of place and at odds with the history and interpretation of the Holocaust. Yet it offers little more than hollow decoration – few will pause to view and contemplate contemporary art in an environment that is designed to crush the spirit rather than send it soaring. According to some commentators, such history and art works are not compatible (see, for example, Richards, 1993). The Holocaust for some remains a vacuum that consumes all light intended to illuminate it.

Technology and particularly multimedia have been used to relate the visitor experience to the individual. The ID card/passport is instrumental in linking the visitors to an individual who actually lived through/died as part of the Holocaust. In this museum, technology is user-friendly to encourage identity updates of the passport individual. These can be printed out at various points and referencing can relate to an individual, time period or an event (Schwartz, 1993). Technology is defining the reality of the visitor's experience. As the museum's Director of Information Systems noted :

We wanted to create a way for them to tailor their private experience . . . There is no way to define the average visitor experience in this kind of museum. Some people have a lot of background and some can't even point to Europe on the globe. (Halery, quoted in Schwartz, 1993, p. 5)

As a museum this has not been short of controversy. Inevitably criticisms of Judaeocentric/partisan versions of the Second World War's history have been levelled from sources such as the revisionist *Journal of Historical Review* (see, for example, O'Keefe, 1995). Yet the opening ceremony itself with its strong representation from Central and Eastern European countries allowed a number of Eastern Europe dignitaries to open up a debate on the role of the Soviet forces following the Second World War, and uncertainty in respect of current Russian foreign policy (Borowiec, 1993, p. 1).

The primary purpose of the museum is often defined by curators and managers as educational, to make visitors understand how attempts to annihilate an entire people came to be and how it was executed (Weinberg, Holocaust Museum Director, quoted in *The Economist*, 1993). It is literally a reminder of the dark side of human nature. As the Director of Public Information commented:

It's a counterpoint to all of these other museums and memorials that you see, they all celebrate humans – their technology and art and creativity and we're saying watch out there is another side to humankind and to what humans are also capable of doing . . . I think people are interested in seeing things and learning things they feel they should see and that's part of it, this is actually something people feel they should see or learn something about or have a responsibility to learn about. (Eskenazi, 1994a, p. 11).

Indeed, the level of interest has been considerable as visitor statistics for the first year of operation indicate (see Table 9.1):

Table 9.1   April 1993–April 1994 visitor statistics, US
            Holocaust Memorial Museum

Group	Number
Number of visitors to the Museum	2,000,000
Number of visitors to the Permanent Exhibition	1,300,000
Average number of groups visiting the Museum daily	24
Number of school groups	3,000
Number of requests for teaching material and assistance filled by the Education Department	36,000
Number of Charter Members	250,000

(*Source*: US Holocaust Memorial Museum, 1996)

Ultimately, then, this is a highly successful project built with private donations on federal land. The US Government remains the ultimate authority and thus influence was observed during the first year of operation when the two senior members of the memorial council administration were replaced (since they were appointments of the former Republican President). Others have identified the presence of the Croatian President, Franjo Tudjman, at the opening ceremony as evidence of this influence. His revisionist views on the Holocaust are well known yet his presence as a guest of honour was viewed as a political necessity (Moskowitz, 1993). As with all museums, the effectiveness of the educational mission of the US Holocaust Memorial Museum has been questioned and its effectiveness in relation to its development cost of $168 million (Levine, 1993). The extent to which the holocaust has been Americanized to infer greater meaning to the largely US audiences has been the subject of debate. As Berenbaum has argued:

In America . . . we recast the story of the Holocaust to teach fundamental American values. What are the fundamental values? For example – when America is at its best – pluralism, democracy, restraint on government, the inalienable rights of individuals, the inability of governments to enter into freedom of religion . . . the Holocaust can become a symbolic orienting event in human history that can prevent recurrence. (Berenbaum, Project Director, US Holocaust Memorial Museum, quoted in Gourevitch, 1993, p. 55)

In this sense memory has been made relative to the USA yet the Jewish Holocaust was a uniquely European event. In some commentators' views, to compare this with the USA, serves only to distort perception by presenting the Holocaust as some form of therapeutic mass cultural experience (Gourevitch, 1993). Yet the actions of the museum's interpretative staff was deliberate. As the Director of Public Information commented:

Well, we have to tell the whole story, but it's pretty Americanized in that it opens with an American at liberation, liberating one of the camps, it was the Soviets that did that, but we needed to start with that connection, it actually starts in the elevator as you heard when you go up with the soldier. This was an actual American soldier who was at the camp, you see the soldiers on the video as you walk in, and you start the story in 1945 with the Americans. Then you go back in history, you have that quotation from Eisenhower too, right at the beginning, then you go back and you start with 1933 and you wind your way back to 45 where we have the full story of liberation and its aftermath. But as you go through it, we tell the story of the *St. Louis*, the ship came in and we did not allow it onto our shores, where the US and Western allies did not allow, we have the bombing of the camps, their refusal to bomb, and there's still an ongoing debate. But there are lessons to be learned there. I don't know if you guys remember Mondale during the debate over accepting the boat people from Vietnam and he made a reference to the Wannsee conference so these things have a relevance to what's going on today with refugees and people that are trying to escape political oppression or some kind of oppression. So there are lessons to be learned there. They're not there to criticize, *per se*, they are there because that is the history of the event, with the idea that we can learn from history and those mistakes will not be repeated. We tried to lay out the history in a straightforward manner, telling the US role, both the positive and the negative, and we end up in the end with the liberation and the survivors coming to our country. (Eskenazi, 1994b, p. 13)

Yet opening the museum through US eyes immediately identifies the US participants as heroes. This, coupled with the attempt to individualize the experience through the use of the ID admission card, can blur the understanding of the museum-goer. The danger here is that interpretation, since it confuses history and utilizes techniques to maintain interest, will remove the real that much farther from the simulation. A distance which Levi referred to as a gap in reality, 'the gap that exists and grows wider every year between things as they were "down there" and things as they are represented by the current imagination fed by approximative books, films, and myths' (Levi, quoted in Gourevitch, 1993, p. 58). The reality gap is the use of the ID card and should not be overlooked. During the Holocaust Jews scrambled to obtain false, non-Jewish papers in order to survive. Here ironically the reverse is in operation, predominantly US visitors enter the museum and leave with Jewish 'identities'. Here thus is the problem in using the Holocaust or any aspect of it as a metaphor. This level of human suffering cannot be a metaphor for anything, and the more it becomes one, the more it becomes removed from the reality.

The use of strong imagery and graphic material or video monitors (protected by a privacy wall to exclude young children) has also evoked a strong response. Lanzmann's views on how familiarity with such images harden the viewer comes to mind. The other criticisms revolve around why people would want to watch this material and, indeed, want to go through this visitor experience. The US Holocaust Memorial Museum's own research shows the visitor behaviour pattern to be highly reverential in behaviour, predominantly education-oriented, and willing to spend up to three hours in this location. In comparison to a norm of one and a half hours for a museum visit, visitors to the US Holocaust Memorial Museum will spend between three and three and a half hours in the museum (Eskenazi, 1994b). As the Director of Public Information noted:

We thought visitors would read the headlines and the large type, scan the material to get a sense of what was there and move on. People are reading everything and watching the whole reel on the monitor and they're taking everything in. Many people are spending four or five hours to go through . . . (Eskenazi, 1994b, p. 7)

In educational terms, museum research points out that 88 per cent of visitors possessed some form of college education, including 71 per cent with a college degree or more and 38 per cent with postgraduate work or beyond. Interestingly, their earnings indicated that some 58 per cent had household incomes of $40,000 (Eskenazi, 1994a). Perhaps most telling is the relatively high proportion of visitors (over 60 per cent) who indicated an intention to return (ibid.).

This museum succeeds in providing an extensive historical narrative of the Holocaust and offers a cogent memorial to its victims. Indeed, the interpretation is clearly superior to the ideologically biased and relatively primitive work found at many of the 'real' sites in Poland, for example. Yet museums are obliged to win and reward the attention of the visitor. Museums are an entertainment form as well as an educative one. If the unimaginable, grotesque and violent are central to American society's post-emotional state (in which deep identification with the suffering and pain of others beyond the immediate family circle is impossible), then this museum provide these amply (Mestrovic, 1996).

Such imagery is darkly fascinating and seductive. Furthermore the educative mission is far from proven. Simply put: Is exposure to barbarism an antidote to that very barbarism? As Gourevitch concluded:

One way history is doomed to repetition at the Holocaust museum is that day in and day out, year after year, the videos of the *Einsatzgruppen* murders will play over and over. There, just off the National Mall in Washington, the victims of Nazism will be on view for the American public, stripped, herded into ditches, shot, buried, and then the tape will repeat and they will be herded into the ditches again, shot again, buried again. I cannot comprehend how anyone can enthusiastically present this constant cycle of slaughter, either as a memorial to those whose deaths are exposed or as an edifying spectacle for the millions of visitors a year who will be exposed to them. Didn't these people suffer enough the first time their lives were taken from them? (Gourevitch, 1993, p. 62)

Indeed, the world fifty years after the Holocaust does not seem restrained by the world fifty years before. Yet this is a story of great human importance that warns all who enter. Indeed, the concourse level in the

US Holocaust Memorial Museum during 1994 featured a gallery of thought-provoking analogous images of ethnic cleansing in the former Yugoslavia (entitled 'Faces of Sorrow : Agony in the Former Yugoslavia, 1994). The similarities of 'cleansing' a society of 'foreign' elements, the re-emergence of age-old hatreds and the rise of xenophobic nationalism have a clear resonance. Such exhibitions clearly reaffirm the US Holocaust Memorial Museum's mission to relate the history of the Holocaust to current world events.

This institution succeeds because it combines memorial with museum and has been commissioned by an act of government. Rarely does any state commemorate its crimes, it is primarily enacted by surviving former victims or their relatives. In the case of the monument to the Civil Rights Movement in Montgomery, Alabama, this was commissioned by the Southern Poverty Law Center (the chronicle/prosecution of civil rights cases) and later endorsed by the State. Thus the government was able to provide the distance between themselves and past crimes (cf. Young, 1993). As Young asks:

> Only rarely does a nation call upon itself to remember the victims of crimes it has perpetrated. Where are the national monuments to the genocide of American Indians, to the millions of Africans enslaved and murdered, to the Russian Kulaks and peasants starved to death by the millions? They barely exist. (Young, 1993, p. 21)

The fate of the Native Americans and the plight of African Americans will be also commemorated on this famous mall of galleries and museums in Washington, DC. But the critique offered that the US Holocaust Memorial Museum should cover other acts of genocide is both simplistic and unrealistic. To create (as was proposed during the development period) a Hall of Genocide, would have been macabre and confusing. However, as a criticism, it is understandable though misdirected. Perhaps more pertinent though is the relatively uncritical treatment of the State of Israel from its creation to its troubled relationship with the Palestinians and their questionable human rights record in the period of recent history.

Yet non-controversial memorials themselves become invisible very quickly. As Musil wrote:

There is nothing in this world as invisible as a monument . . . they are no doubt erected to be seen – indeed, to attract attention. But at the same time they are impregnated with something that repels attention, causing the glance to roll right off . . . (Musil, quoted in Wieseltier, 1993, p. 19)

This difference is apparent in the comparison of visitor interest in the 'official' Kennedy cenotaph and the Sixth Floor; the countless monuments to the UK First World War dead and the 'Trench Experience' of the UK's Imperial War Museum. It is the contrast of spectacle and theatre with an interpretation of history via a lifeless form. The US Holocaust Memorial Museum provides shock in its format, building, design and content. In telling the tale the museum creates and reinforces the monument. This public space dispels the banality of so many other figures, markers and interpretative forums.

Maya Lin's nearby Vietnam Veterans Monument with its abstract modernist commemoration, so radically different from typical figurational monuments, will remain the primary US anti-memorial but it will be analogous to the US Holocaust Memorial Museum which offers a vision of the past that is both critical and radical in its treatment.

Tragedy and opportunity

The war in the former Yugoslavia has already spawned its own forms of dark tourism. Tourists already travel to Sarajevo to gaze at sites of some of the worst aspects of the conflict (O'Reilly, 1996). Tours incorporate the notorious sniper alley (the main street where many civilians were killed) and the site of the slaughter of twenty-one persons next to the Catholic Cathedral. Guides show tourists the ruined Olympic stadium, the battle-scarred mosque and other tragic reminders of this war.

The justification from such tourists is usually couched in understanding and education about this war which has claimed at least 200,000 civilians. Yet the macabre reality of tourists purchasing spent shell casings, shrapnel and bullets as mementoes on what has become known as the 'massacre trail' is that they are simply pursuing the dark history of recent events. The immediacy of the tragedy and the relative 'closeness' of the conflict have similarly attracted them in the same way as 25 Cromwell Street attracted many visitors to the UK's most recent site of multiple murder. As one US tourist visiting Sarajevo defended her holiday:

> Sure, I was there to see what happened in the war. What's wrong with that? It is interesting. People look round American Civil War battlegrounds and nobody complains. I went to France to see where my grandfather fought at D-Day. I guess this is more recent but the principle is the same . . . (McGill, quoted in O'Reilly, 1996, p. 3)

The Sarajevo travel company, Centrotrans, is currently negotiating to fly Turkish visitors into Bosnia-Herzegovina twice per week to visit this tragic capital. A representative of the company, when challenged that this was pure exploitation of a recent site of death, purely for financial reward, countered: 'Look, I am from the city and I lived here during the war. Do you think I would help people get some twisted pleasure from our suffering?' (ibid., p. 6). Similar plans have been proposed for the development of the Croatian region of Konavia. Here the historical sites of Cilip and the surrounding regions have been identified as a reoriented attraction which can demonstrate the impact of twentieth-century warfare. Literally to reconstruct the deconstructed (Desin, 1995).

The parallel with Taxi and City Bus 'tours of the living history' which are offered in Northern Ireland is clearly apparent. These offer tourists a perspective on the recent past (and the present) political turmoil which has erupted into conflict over the past quarter of a century. These tours had their historical origins in the cease-fire of 1995 and they offer to Belfast visitors a perspective on recent civil unrest which is studiously avoided in tours of Ulster Museum and Belfast City Hall. The City Bus 'Living History Tour', is perhaps worth further consideration. This tour runs on Tuesdays, Thursdays and Sundays, 9.30 a.m. and 2.00 p.m. It is a three and a half hour tour of the famous death sites of Northern Ireland, dealing with the recent past and the troubles. It is operated by the City Bus Company, and is essentially a state-operated company. Demand is so great that all potential customers must arrive one hour before commencement. Currently they do not have the bus stock to cope with demand for the tours. In 1996 it was planned to operate an increased fleet over a seven-day period. Notably bookings and information on the tour could be made through the Belfast Tourist Information Centre, thus ensuring its 'legitimate' operation as the state-approved tour. Private operators are controlled and restrained at a civic level by road traffic planners and through delays with insurance, etc. So essentially, the only legitimate tour visitors can take is the City Bus 'Living History Tour'. Private operators are essentially restrained by administration. The only real competition comes from the 'black cabs' whose operation remains associated with the paramilitary organizations. The cabs can be located outside of Belfast City Hall and after negotiation will provide the passenger with a tour of some of the trouble spots. As a passenger on such a tour, one of the authors visited both Protestant and Catholic housing estates to view celebrated murals. Time was provided to exit the cab and photograph places of soldiers' deaths, etc. Historically, details are sometimes vague but demand (at least during the cease-fire) was brisk. Yet such a tour is viewed as 'illegitimate' by tourist information centre staff. Indeed, during the time of the cease-fire TIC staff were inviting tourists to either take York guide taxis (a legitimate alternative) or to walk the famous sites of North Belfast (Shankhill) and West Belfast (Falls Road). Tourists were encouraged to view 'unusual' sites such as Springfield Road police station: '. . . not like the kind of police station you've been used to' (TIC counter staff to author).

CHAPTER TEN

The Future of Dark Tourism: From the Final Solution to the End of History

Increasingly, tourism professionals are expected to contribute to the development of visitor experiences that emanate from 'dark' events or sites. Historians, or more correctly histographers, are well aware of the difficulty of objectivity and the concomitant epistemological, methodological and ideological content of any 'histories' produced within their discipline. Viewing the past – as opposed to history – as a set of discourses aimed at a particular group (in this case tourists) highlights the suggestion that history is for someone and that the contemporary dominant power élites are most likely to play a significant part in shaping that reality when the target group is ordinary citizens in the guise of tourists. Thus, those with responsibilities for tourism promotion and development may have a previously unrecognized ethical dilemma – that of adjudicating in debates over 'whose history' prevails in interpretation. While the resolution of the dilemma may seem relatively obvious in a case such as the Channel Islands (see Chapter 5), where widely publicized new information sources shed an alternative light upon the occupation and thus called previous interpretations into question, it is evident that, elsewhere, comparable 'inaccuracies' or inappropriate biases may dominate tourism products.

In the case where the recent past is becoming the province of tourism as much as histography and where museum and heritage resource managers are viewing schools' twentieth-century history as a source of market growth, tourism professionals may need to become sensitized to the presentation of 'alternative pasts' at their sites rather than offering only one view of the past. Further research is needed to explore where the role of the historian ends and that of the tourist site manager begins in the interpretation of alternative, recent pasts.

Many of the events considered within the purview of dark tourism have entered the curricula of modern history in the liberal democratic world, providing both further discourse upon the events themselves and encouraging future visitors to some sites – whether in organized trips designed to enliven learning strategies or in tourist experiences later in life. Thus, education itself may have become a key element in transmitting and securing an interest in these events, in ways which could become at least as effective as the technological dimensions discussed in Chapters 1 and 2. Events such as the Jewish Holocaust in Germany, Vietnam and Black Civil Rights in schools in the USA, the conduct of the imperial government during the Second World War in Japan and the Irish Question in Ulster and mainland UK have all been reappraised recently as elements of the students' education about aspects of their national heritage which may have been suppressed, or represented differently in the 'approved' version. Shifts from national embarrassment over past conduct to public admission and acknowledgement of reprehensible policies may be presented as evidence of emerging tolerance, rationality and progress within the Enlightenment project associated with the Western world as influenced by the Judaeo-Christian religions. However, they also present entrepreneurial opportunities, which have not been lost upon site managers and developers.

In some cases these effectively 'Western' values are commodified and represented at sites located within the value system itself. Where this prevailing value system is challenged by alternatives such as Islam or (so-called) New Age philosophies *inter alia*, it is less clear what will be the outcome. Thus, it is fair to say that the analysis offered in this book is fundamentally Eurocentric and 'Western'. The non-representation of the Tiananmen Square tragedy in China may be more a reflection of dominant political values currently in place. Where remembrance is both possible and encouraged in some parts of Asia, such as in the Museum of Human Genocide in Phnom Penh and where commodification of death has occurred, such as at the Cu Chi tunnels near Ho Che Minh City in Vietnam, the type and tone of interpretation appear to have, at least, an eye upon the probability that many of the most economically desirable visitors will originate from the political West and, thus, tends to ignore some of the responsibility of certain Western democracies in the prosecution of these conflicts. Nevertheless, where many of the most lucrative market segments in a global tourist industry originate from liberal democratic states, there are political and economic imperatives to capitalize quickly upon notoriety, whether within Europe (e.g. parts of Croatia, Sarajevo, trips to Bucharest based upon accommodation in Ceauşescu's former palace and travel using his vehicles) or beyond.

Events for the early part of the twentieth century and at the far end of what we have chosen to term 'chronological distance' are being said to be moving from memory into history. The First World War and acts of associated remembrance of those who died have reached the eightieth anniversary of its end as this book is being completed. As these milestones of chronological distance are completed, anniversaries of events at junctures, which are products of five, and particularly ten, years ago begin to assume media-led and touristic significance far in excess of their actual importance. Thus, the thirtieth anniversary of the assassination of Kennedy, the fiftieth anniversary of the D-Day landings in Normandy, the fiftieth anniversary of the bombing of Hiroshima and Nagasaki and the eightieth anniversary of the end of the First World War, have led to major media coverage and increases in visitation to the appropriate sites – which, itself, leads to yet more media coverage of the veterans and other interested parties in their visits. Inevitably, increased travel and visits are 'good news' for the local tourism industry – and lead to an imperative to capitalize upon impending anniversaries from managers of the sites themselves (cf. the Sixth Floor, Dallas).

A growing number of experiences are being offered to tourists which could be said to recreate 'last journeys' in space and real time and these raise questions of both taste and sanctity. We referred earlier to the possibility of undertaking John F. Kennedy's last journey in a Lincoln Continental identical to that in which he was assassinated. More recently, and to the derision of the British media, a Paris agency offers the prospect of following the final route of Diana, Princess of Wales, through the streets of the city in a black S-class Mercedes Benz, identical to that in which she died. The recency of the death of Diana, Princess of Wales, and the apparent sanctity of her memory leading to what the UK *Guardian* newspaper described as an 'oppression of grief' gave rise to criticisms based upon assertions of inappropriate exploitation. What is at issue in both of these cases is doubt and anxiety over the commodification of the journeys – presumably, some individuals may follow these routes daily in pursuit of their personal business and some tourists may, in their own vehicles, trace the route. Once commodified, the 'dark' explicit concerns become evident. Taken a stage further, and stimulated by the success of the recent film *Titanic*, voyages from New York and Boston which recreate not the last journey (which originated from Southampton) but the 'experience' of the last journey of the SS *Titanic* through consumption of identical music, meals and 'enter-tainment', etc., to those offered on the doomed vessel were reported recently in the UK press. The destination of these voyages was the site of the wreck of the *Titanic*, above which a Christian ceremony was conducted prior to returning to port.

At the edge of the territory in which the internal nature of the terms of modernity's own demise are graphically interpreted and commodified as tourist products are sites and situations where science is called into question – and, sometimes, its demise is the spur for tourism. Sites such as the proposed Dynamic Earth Centre in Edinburgh, Disney's US EPCOT Centre and various representations of the Rainforest (such as that in New Orleans) all contain evidence of, and warnings about, the effects of maintaining unsustainable lifestyles based upon consumption,

36   *Vehicle used for Graveline Tours at Mann's Chinese Theater, Los Angeles*

planned obsolescence and pollution. Governmental and commercial sites throughout Arizona and New Mexico, where once the weapons and industrial development of atomic mass destruction were contained have increasingly been opened to the general public spawning the term 'atomic tourism' to describe this phenomena. Like the SS *Titanic*, the First World War and the Jewish Holocaust, these sites sit at the cusp of modernity and post-modernity where public doubts over the 'solutions' they offered and the mastery of natural forces they implied have been commodified via the complicity of global communication technology industries into a tourist product.

The raw and the cooked

A number of instances sited in the previous section indicate that the distinction between the actual site of death and disaster and the subsequent re-presentation of that event at the site itself, or at another site, or in another manner has become a matter of continued negotiation. Thus, it has become possible to think in terms of interpreting a 'dark' event at another site, possibly far removed from the original location. However, there are problems within sites themselves which call into question the boundaries of reality and representation. Battle sites such as those of the Somme offensive in 1916 stretch over many hectares which were rapidly returned to agricultural production immediately upon the aftermath of the First World War. The sites of battle as presented to visitors in the late twentieth century, which include cemeteries and visitor centres, represent only a fraction of the complete battlefield. It is therefore inevitable that some parts of the battlefield are neither presented as such nor are accorded similar reverence as the 'official sites' of remembrance and interpretation. Provided that visitors collude in this celebration of the non-authentic it is unlikely that the ethics of the decisions made in 1918 will be questioned. Where greater political significance is accorded to other sites, similar problems of authenticity and the 'real' persist. At Oswieczim, the Auschwitz–Birkenau complex of slave labour and execution camps stretched across a far greater area of land than that which is now accorded as a site of remembrance and visitation (see earlier discussion in Chapter 4). The integrity of these sites is jealously guarded by pressure groups while areas outside of the 'authentic' site have undergone considerable industrial and commercial development. Thus some 'dark' sites have become abbreviated as part of the commodification process, presumably as a result of pragmatism in both industrial and agricultural planning but, nevertheless, becoming rather less than that which they purport to represent. At the very least, the reverence which some of these sites invite should also be accorded to surrounding landscapes. Such an approach, however, would lead to significant problems of land use planning which would be inconvenient in the development of tourism and other industries. If the approaches being adopted are not intentionally deceptive, then they are guilty of not airing the expediencies of touristic site development in the information provided to visitors.

In questioning the way in which interpretation of events has been handled and managed and in being sceptical about the boundaries of site, event and representation, it is inevitable that questions about the 'official version' of some events are raised. One such event being the celebrated sighting of an unidentified flying object at Roswell, New Mexico, in 1946, the source of late twentieth-century preoccupations about extraterrestrial visitation and allegations of governmental collusion in a cover-up. In turn, these events have fuelled media interest from the cinematic which purports to relate the 'true' story (i.e. *The Roswell Incident*) to the documentary and televisual/fictional (e.g. *The X Files, Dark Skies*). Central to all of these accounts and representations is the element of distrust in government, rather than, necessarily, the threat from extraterrestrial beings (or their metaphoric Communist infiltrationist counterparts). Interest in Roswell appears to belie the US Government's assertion that the object in question was a weather balloon. Thus, a non-event, at least by 'official' standards, and its representation in the media have led to a growing level of visitation to Roswell and a number of other sites with similar backgrounds and the commodification, once again, of public anxiety and doubt. Of equal significance is the presentation of what might have been (but was not) in the form of re-presentation. At various sites in the UK, underground villages which would have housed key politicians and officials in the event of a nuclear holocaust have been decommissioned and sold to tourist developers. These are mostly offered into tourist markets under the title of the 'secret bunker', showing how life might have been for those who would have been underground. In a number of cases such developments simulate the noise and vibration effects of nuclear strikes at a variety of UK sites.

If non-events can be considered within the analysis of dark tourism, then what of the selection, and more importantly, the non-selection of certain events for presentation within touristic products? Why are some events more likely to receive such treatment rather than others? If suspicion of government is a key element of these products, then why has the Watergate building in Washington, DC, not exploited its connection with one of the USA's most significant political scandals? If the oppression of communities or ethnic groups is so important, then why is there so little interpretation of the atrocities committed against the Roma peoples from 1945 and most particularly in Central and Eastern Europe since the fall of the Berlin Wall? In some cases governments are moved to prevent possibilities of exploitation of notorious sites, believing this to be in the best interests of the public and to the relatives of the victims. One recent example would be the government-sponsored demolition of 25 Cromwell Road, Gloucester, UK, where Fred and Rosemary West tortured and murdered several young people.

It has not escaped our notice that dark tourism commodities have been associated not only with mass death and destruction, often where the main tenets of modernity have been called into question, but also with the death of celebrated individuals, commodified in life as 'stars', fuelled by media interest and public prurience. Re-enactment of the last ride of James Dean in contemporary costume and on the anniversary of his death at Cholame appears to have been a spontaneous act of remembrance by loyal fans – epitomized by the erection of a memorial to Dean's death by a Japanese businessman, rather than a local touristic imperative. However, other individuals, notably John F. Kennedy and Diana, Princess of Wales, have spawned fascination and public ownership in death which has almost eclipsed their lives. This kind of fascination appears to be an aspect of the commodification of these individuals as icons via the media. At the same time the communications technologies which have played such a part in developing interest in the phenomena have in turn been presented as elements of 'dark tourism products'. They in turn offer further stimulus for the developer keen to exploit the commercial potential. Recent successful films such as *Titanic* (1997) and *Saving Private Ryan* (1998) presented possibilities for developers associated with the events portrayed. More importantly, new technologies emerge which themselves stimulate interest in sites such as former atomic research, development and military installations, etc. The accessibility and relative 'openness' of the Internet allow for the possibility of all types of opinion to be aired, including some which may directly challenge prevailing orthodoxies.

What, then, has been the effect of such academic discourse in this field? Has such research in the pursuit of scholarly goals led to a further commodification of the academic study of this type of subject? Perhaps issues which some would rather not have been raised will lead to further development and academic 'exploitation' of this field. It is perhaps too easy to endorse the *status quo* on certain types of interpretation – the impossibility and unacceptability of criticism in some arenas, for example, the Jewish Holocaust. If further research is inevitable then it is visitor motivation that represents an important aspect of 'understanding' and perhaps also the effects upon victims and the relatives of victims compared to the 'casual' dark tourist.

Bibliography

Aguirre, R. (1988) 'Family objections won't halt JFK exhibit', *Dallas Times Herald*, 63, p. 3.

Akis, S. and Warner, J. (1994) 'Reports – a descriptive analysis of North Cyprus', *Tourism Management*, Vol. 15, No. 5, pp. 370–400.

Altinay, M. and Biçak A. (1997) 'Competitive strategies for the tourism sector of a small island state: the case of North Cyprus', *Journal of Vacation Marketing*, Vol. 4, No. 2, pp. 136–44.

Andronicou, A. (1979) *'Tourism: Passport to Development?'*, Oxford: Oxford University Press/World Bank/UNESCO.

Ascherson, N. (1995) 'Remains of the abomination', in *The Independent on Sunday*, 22 January, pp. 12–16.

Ashworth, G. (1996) 'Holocaust tourism and Jewish culture: the lessons of Krakow–Kazimierz', in Robinson, M., Evans, N. and Callaghan, P. (eds) *Tourism and Culture: Towards the 21st Century*, London: Athenaeum Press.

Associated Press (1988) 'Kennedy friends upset by Museum plans', *Dallas Times Herald*, 61, p. 1.

Atkinson, R. (1993) 'Holocaust Museum spurs renewal history debate', in *The Washington Post*, 24 June, p. 3.

Avisar, I. (1988) *Screening the Holocaust: Cinemas Images of the Unimaginable*, Bloomington: Indiana University Press.

Avisar, I. (1989) *Screening the Holocaust*, Bloomington and Indianapolis: Indiana University Press.

Barthes, R. (1981) *Camera Lucide: Reflections on Photography*, trans. R. Howard, New York: Hill & Wang.

Baudrillard, J. (1983) *Simulations*, New York: Semiotext.

Baudrillard, J. (1988) *The Evil Demon of Images*, Sidney: Power Institute Publications.

Bauman, Z. (1995) *Modernity and the Holocaust*, Cambridge: Polity Press.

Begley, L. (1993) *Wartime Lies*, London: Picador.

Berenbaum, l. (1993) in Gourevitch, P. 'Behold now Behemoth', in *Harpers Magazine*, May, pp. 55–62.

Berman, M. (1983) *All That is Solid Melts into Air*, London: Verso.

Biçak, A. and Altinary, M. (1996) 'Economic impact of the Israeli tourists on North Cyprus', *Annals of Tourism Research*, Vol. 23, No. 4, pp. 928–31.

Bletchley Park Trust (1995a) *Bletchley Park: Britain's Best Kept Secret*, Bletchley Park Trust.

Bletchley Park Trust (1995b) *Bletchley Park: World War II Codebreaking*, Bletchley Park Trust.

Bohm-Duchen, M. (1995) *After Auschwitz: Responses to the Holocaust in Contemporary Art*, Sunderland: Northern Centre for Contemporary Art.

Boonstra, J., Jansen, H. and Kniesmeyer, J. (1993) *Antisemitism: A History Potrayed*, The Hague: SDU.

Boonstra, J. and Rijnders, M. J. (1992) *Anne Frank House: A Museum with a Story*, The Hague: SDU.

Boorman, D. (1988) *At the Going Down of the Sun: British First World War Memorials*, London: William Sessions Ltd.

Bordage, R. (1993) 'Sachsenhausen: a flawed museum', in *Museum International*, Vol. 45, pp. 26–31.

Borowiec, A. (1993) 'No shortage of controversy at opening', *The Washington Times*, 23 April, p. 1.

Borowski, T. (1992) 'This way for the gas, ladies and gentlemen', *Short Stories*, Harmondsworth: Penguin.

Boston Globe, The (1995) '50 years later, Okinawa evokes painful memories, signs of healing', Saturday, 24 June.

Britain at War Experience (no date) *Marketing brochure*, Britain at War Experience.

Broadcast Magazine (1963) 'Comments on coverage: well done', 2 December, p. 50.

Brookner, A. (1995) *Latecomers*, London: Flamingo.

Bull, A. (1995) *Strange Angels*, London: Black Swan.

Bunting, M. (1995) *The Model Occupation*, London: HarperCollins.

Burkhart, A. and Medlik, S. (1981) *Tourism, Past, Present and Future*, London: Heinemann.

Calhoun, R. (1968) 'JFK Museum ideas gets mixed views', in *Dallas Times Herald*, 16 December, p. 1, p. 28.

Caseby, R. and Goldman, S. (1994) 'A terrible past revisited', *The Sunday Times*, The Culture, 23 March, pp. 2–4.

Cesarani, D. (ed.) (1994) *The Final Solution*, London: Routledge.

Chicago, J. (1993) *Holocaust Project: From Darkness to Light*, Harmondsworth: Penguin.

City Plan of Lefkoşa (1997) *Tourism Promotion Brochure*, Turkish Republic of North Cyprus.

Coad, J. G. (no date) *Hellfire Corner*, London: English Heritage.

Collins, J. (1989) 'JFK assassination exhibit nears opening on the sixth floor', *Dallas Times Herald*, 20 May, p. 1.

Connally, J. (1988) quoted in '25th anniversary of JFK's assassination', *Night Line*, ABC News, quoted in B. Zelizer (1992).

Coombs, R. E. B. (1994) *Before Endeavours Fade: A Guide to the Battlefields of the First World War*, London: Battle of Britain Prints International.

Cooper, C., Fletcher, J., Gilbert, D. and Wanhill, S. (1993) *Tourism Principles and Practice*, London: Pitman.

Council for British Archaeology (no date) *The Defence of Britain Project*, London: The Council for British Archaeology.

Cruickshank, C. (1975) *The German Occupation of the Channel Islands*, Oxford: Oxford University Press.

Dallas County Historical Foundation (1989) *The Sixth Floor. John F. Kennedy and the Memory of a Nation*, Dallas, Texas.

Dallas County Historical Foundation (1994a) *Fact Sheet: the Sixth floor*, Dallas, Texas: The Sixth Floor press release.

Dallas County Historical Foundation (1994b) *Documentary History: The Story of the 'Sixth Floor'*, Dallas, Texas: The Sixth Floor press release.

Dallas County Historical Foundation (1994c) *History and the Significance of the Landmark District*, Dallas, Texas: The Sixth Floor press release.

Dallas County Historical Foundation (1994d) *Dealey Plaza – National Historic Landmark District Factsheet*, Dallas, Texas: The Sixth Floor press release.

Dallas County Historical Foundation (1994e) *The Sixth Floor Museum Records Banner Year*, Dallas, Texas: The Sixth Floor press release.

Dallas County Historical Foundation (1994f) *Inside The Sixth Floor: What the Permanent Historical Exhibition Contains*, Dallas, Texas: The Sixth Floor Press Release.

Dallas County Historical Foundation (1994g) *Awards and Distinctions*, Dallas, Texas: The Sixth Floor Press Release.

Dallas County Historical Foundation (1994h) *Questions and Answers*, Dallas, Texas: The Sixth Floor press release.

Davies, P. (1990) *All Played Out*, London: Heinemann.

Day Visitors Guide to Alderney (1995) Alderney Tourist Board.

Desin, M. (1995) 'Tour of Duty', *Leisure Opportunities*, 22 March, pp. 36–7.

Deuchar, S. (1996) 'Sense and sensitivity: appraising the *Titanic*', *International Journal of Heritage Studies*, Vol. 2, No. 4, pp. 212–21, Intellect.

Directory of Holocaust Institutions, Washington D.C (1995) Washington, DC: US Holocaust Memorial Council.

Dodd, C. H. (1995) *The Cyprus Issue – A Current Perspective*, 2nd edition, Huntingdon: The Eothen Press.

Donat, A. (1965) *The New Kingdom*, New York: Holt, Reinhart & Winston.

Douglas, R. (1994) Interview with the Dallas Chamber of Commerce, Dallas, Texas, undertaken by the authors, November.

Drake C. (1997), 'Quality tours widen horizons on the island of Cyprus', *The European*, 3 April, p. 25 [1], http://web4.searchbank.com/infotrac/session/987/463/1388446W1/54!xrn_60.

Dresden, S. (1995) *Persecution, Extermination, Literature*, Toronto: Toronto University Press.

Dwork, D. and Van Pelt, J. (1994) 'Reclaiming Auschwitz', in Hartman, G. H. (ed.) *Holocaust Rememberance: The Shapes of Memory*, Oxford: Blackwell.

Eco, U. (1986) *Travels in Hyperreality*, London: Picador.

Economist, The (1993) Editorial, 'Holocaust museum never again', 1 May, p. 118.

Economist, The (1997) 'The Cyprus timebomb', 1 November, p. 18.

Economist, The (1998a) 'Can the circle be squared?', 21 February, p. 2 and pp. 46–51.

Economist, The (1998b) 'The king of Turkish Cyprus', 21 February, p. 51.

Enever, T. (1995) *Britain's Best Kept Secret: Ultra's Base at Bletchley Park*, Strong: Alan Sutton Publishing.

English Heritage (1994) *English Heritage Monitor*, London: The Agency.

English Tourist Board (1994) *Marketing the Arts in Tourism*, London: The English Tourist Board.

Esheim, S. (1995) *Unwelcome Strangers*, New York: Oxford University Press.

Eskenazi, S. (1994a) Interview with Director of Public Information, US Holocaust Memorial Museum, Washington, DC, by the authors.

Eskenazi, S. (1994b) *Summary of Results of Museum Visitors Survey, US Holocaust Memorial Museum, Washington DC*, Document for public information (press briefing document, 11 February 1994).

Evans, D. (1994) *A Guide to the Beaches and Battlefields of Normandy*, London: Michael Joseph.

Evans, M. M. (1992) *Ypres in War and Peace*, London: Pitkin.

Faces of Sorrow – Agony in the former Yugolsavia (1994) Publicity leaflet of photography exhibition presented by the US Holocaust Memorial Museum, *Time* Magazine, Life Magazine and Time Inc.

Foley, M. (1995) 'Cultural tourism in the UK', Richards, G. (ed.) *Cultural Tourism in Europe*, Wallinford: CAB.

Foley, M. and Lennon, J. (1995a) 'JFK and cultural tourism', paper presented at First Annual Conference for Popular Culture, Manchester Metropolitan University, Manchester.

Foley, M. and Lennon, J. (1995b) 'War and cultural tourism in Berlin and London', paper presented at conference entitled 'The Urban Environment: Tourism', South Bank University, September.

Foley, M. and Lennon, J. (1996) 'JFK and dark tourism – a fascination with assassination', *International Journal of Heritage Studies*, Vol. 2, No. 4, pp. 198–211.

Foley, M. and Lennon, J. (1997) 'Dark tourism – an ethical dilemma', in Foley, M., Lennon, J. and Maxwell, G. (eds) *Strategic Issues for the Hospitality, Tourism and Leisure Industries*, London: Cassell.

Frank, B. G. (1992) *A Travel Guide to Jewish Europe*, London: Pelican.

Friedlander, S. (1993) *Memory, History and the Extermination of the Jews in Europe*, Bloomington: Indiana University Press.

Gallimard Guides (no date) *Official Guide: The D-Day Landings and the Battle of Normandy*, Paris: Gallimard.

Gedenkstätte und Museum Sachsenhausen (1995) *Barracks 38 and 39*, Oranienburg: Museum Sachsenhausen.

Gilbert, M. (1986) *The Holocaust: The Jewish Tragedy*, London: Collins.

Goldstein, M. (1995) 'The International Council of the Museum', *Pro-Memoria*, Nos 1–2, January, pp. 6–7, Oswieczim.

Gourevitch, P. (1993) 'Behold now Behemoth', *Harpers Magazine*, pp. 55–62.

Gruber, R. E. (1992) *Jewish Heritage Travel (Central and Eastern Europe)*, Chichester: Wiley.

Gruber, R. E. (1993) *Jewish Heritage Travel*, London: Wiley.

Hartman, G. H. (ed.) (1986) *Bitburg in moral and political perspective*, Bloomington: Indiana University Press.

Hartman, G. H. (ed.) (1994) *Holocaust Remembrance: The Shapes of Memory*, Oxford: Blackwell.

Herald, The (1996) 'Tourists in Dunblane asked for tact', 7 August, p. 1.

Herbert, D. T. (ed.) (1995) *Heritage and Tourism*, London: Mansell.

Herrera, J. (1995) Interview with Vice-President of Sales and Marketing – Dallas Visitor and Convention Bureau, 18 November, Dallas, Texas, by the authors.

Holt's Tours (1995) *Battlefields and History, January 1996 to March 1997*, Sandwich: Green Field Leisure.

Hondius, D., Kniesmeyer, J. and van der Wal, B. (1985) *Anne Frank in the World 1929–1945: Pictures and Text of Exhibition*, Amsterdam: Anne Frank Stichting.

Honolulu Advertiser, The (1993) 'It's hard to forgive, some visitors say', Monday, 6 December.

Honolulu Star-Bulletin (1992) 'New Dec. 7 film debuts at Arizona, Thursday', 3 December.

Hoppe, C. (1982) 'Plan envisions JFK museum in depository', *Dallas Morning News*, 7 December, p. 15A.

House of the Wannsee Conference (1992a) *House of the Wannsee Conference: History of the Building*, Berlin (free information pamphlet).

House of the Wannsee Conference (1992b) *House of the Wannsee Conference: History as a Learning Site*, Berlin (free information pamphlet).

Hunt-Jones, C. (1983) quoted in Geddie, T. 'Assassination museum models now on display', *Dallas Daily News*, 19 December, p. 1.

Incoming Guide – Orbis (1994) 'In the footsteps of Poland's Jews', *The Warsaw Voice Polish and Central European Review*, 9 January, No. 2 (272), pp. 14–17.

Insdorf, A. (1989) *Indelible Shadows: Film and the Holocaust*, 2nd edn., Cambridge: Cambridge University Press.

Jackson, L. (1988) '$4 admission proposed for JFK exhibition', *Dallas Morning News*, 15 July, p. 2.

Jersey Tourism (1995a) *An Island of Peace with a History of War*, press release.

Jersey Tourism (1995b) *Liberation Year in Jersey – Fiftieth Anniversary News Round-Up*, press release.

Jersey Tourism (1995c) *Our Dear Channel Islands*, press release.

Jersey Tourism (1995d) *The Fiftieth Anniversary of the Liberation of Jersey 1945–95*, free promotional leaflet.

John F. Kennedy Library (1994) *The New Museum at John F. Kennedy Library*, Columbia Point, Boston MA.

Kagam, J. (1992) *Poland's Jewish Heritage*, New York: Hippocrene.

King, P. (1991) *The Channel Islands War 1940–45*, London: Robert Hale.

Kleiwer, T. and Martin, B. (1971) 'JFK Museum slated for depositing', *Dallas Morning News*, 21 July, p. 3.

Klemke, R. (1995) 'Hitler's war bunker digs up dissent', *Scotland on Sunday*, 26 March, p. 15.

Knapp, S. (1989) 'Collective memory and the actual past', *Representations*, Spring.

Krajewski, S. (1995) 'Commemorating Auschwitz: questions and challenges', *Pro-Memoria*, Nos 1–2, January, pp. 29–33.

Kugelmass, J. (1994) 'Why we go to Poland: Holocaust tourism as secular ritual', in Young, J. E. (ed.) *The Art of Memory: Holocaust Memorials in History*, Munich: Prestel, pp. 175–84.

Kushner, A. (1995) *The Holocaust and the Liberal Imagination*, Washington, DC: Black Publications.

Langer, L. (1975) *The Holocaust and the Literary Imagination*, New Haven, CT: Yale University Press.

Langer, L. (1991) *Holocaust Testimonies – The Ruins of Memory*, New Haven, CT: Yale University Press.

Lanzmann, C. (1995a) 'Why Spielberg has distorted the truth', *The Guardian Weekly*, 3 March, p. 18.

Lanzmann, C. (1995b) *Screening the Holocaust*, Bloomington and Indianapolis: Indiana University Press.

Larson, K. (1993) 'Where does it end?', *New York*, 10 May, pp. 66–7.

Leipeiger, N. (1995) 'Remembrance or oblivion?', in Editor's Mail, *Pro-Memoria*, Nos 1–2, January, p. 71.

Lennon, J. and McPherson, G. (1995) 'Retailing strategies in UK museums and galleries: developing revenue generation strategies', in Armistead, C. and Teare, R. (eds) *Services Management: New Directions and Perspectives*, London: Cassell.

Levi, P. (1986) 'Revisiting the camps', in Young, J. E. (ed.) *The Art of Memory: Holocaust Memorials in History*, Munich: Prestel.

Levi, P. (1990) *The Drowned and the Saved*, London: Abacus.

Levine, H. (1993) 'Never again? The new Holocaust Museum has a difficult role to play', *The Boston Sunday Globe*, 25 April, pp. 69–72.

Lickorish, L. and Jenkins, C. (1997) *An Introduction to Tourism*, Oxford: Butterworth Heinemann.

Linenthal, E. T. (1993) *Sacred Ground: Americans and their Battlefields*, 2nd edition, Urbanba, Ill: University of Illinois Press.

Linenthal, E. T. (1995a) 'Can museums achieve a balance between memory and history?', *The Chronicle of Higher Education*, 10 February, p. 45–68.

Lithenthal, E. T. (1995) *Preserving Memory: The Struggle to Create America's Holocaust Museum'*, London: Viking Penguin.

Lockhart, D. (1994) 'Reports – tourism in North Cyprus: patterns, policies and prospects', *Tourism Management*, Vol. 15, No. 5, pp. 370–8.

Longworth, P. (1985) *The Unending Vigil: A History of the Commonwealth War Graves Commission, 1917–1984*, London: Secker & Warburg.

McCafferty, N. (1995) 'No trouble on magical mystery tour', *Scotland on Sunday*, 16 April, p. 6.

MacWilliam, J. (1995) 'Hitler's war bunker digs up dissent', *Scotland on Sunday*, 26 March, p. 15.

Magee, D. (1995) Interview conducted with Superintendent Don Magee, USS *Arizona* Memorial and Visitor Center, July 1995.

Martin, L. (1991) 'Sixth Floor – a Kennedy Museum', *Dallas Times Herald*, 20 April, p. A16.

Martin, R. (1988) 'Soft-selling the Sixth Floor', *Dallas Observer*, 8 December, p. 7.

Matthews, D. (1987) *The Cyprus Tapes*, London: K. Rusten & Brother.

Mechanicus, P. (1968) *Waiting for Death*, London: Calder & Boyars.

Mestrovic, S. (1996) *Post-Emotional Society*, London: Sage.

Miller, J. (1990) *One by One by One: Facing the Holocaust*, New York: HarperCollins.

Miller, L. (1985) 'Kennedy exhibit plan foundering', *Dallas Morning News*, 22 November, p. 1A.

Milton, S. (1991) *In Fitting Memory: The Art and Politics of Holocaust Memorials*, Detroit: Wayne State University Press.

Minutaglia, B. (1993) 'Quiet healers', *Dallas Life Magazine*, 21 November, pp. 22–8.

Moore, J. (1993) 'Holocaust Museum's campaign to remember', *The Chronicle of Philanthropy*, Vol. V, No. II, pp. 1–30.

Moskowitz, I. (1993) 'The dangers of "Americanizing the Holocaust"', *Jewish Press*, 7 May, p. 36.

Murray, K. (1996) 'Macabre re-enactment lets tourists be JFK for the day', *The Herald*, Glasgow, p. 4.

Museum of Jewish Heritage (1987) *A Living Memorial to the Holocaust'*, New York: Holocaust Memorial Commission.

Musil, M. (1993) in Wieseltier, L. (1993) 'After Memory – Reflection on the Holocaust Memorial Museum', *The New Republic*, 3 May, pp. 16–26.

Needham, D. (1995) Interview with Director of Public Relations, Jersey Tourism, by the authors.

Neilsen Co (1963) 'TV responses to the death of a President', cited in *'World Listened and Watched'*, a special report on broadcasting, 2 December 1963, pp. 36–59.

Noble Caledonian Limited (1998) 'Kyrenia for all seasons', *The Independent on Sunday*, 21 June, p. 50.

North Cyprus (1997) *Tourism Promotion Brochure*, Kryrenia, North Cyprus.

Nowinski, M. (1991) *In Fitting Memory: the Art and Politics of Holocaust Memorials*, Detroit: Wayne State University Press.

O'Keefe T. J. (1995) *The US Holocaust Memorial Museum: A Costly and Dangerous Mistake* (. . . . wan.com/~ihrgreg/pamphlets/ushmm.html)

O'Reilly, D. (1996) 'Massacre trail lures sightseers', *The European*, 14–20 November, p. 3.

Oswieczim Tourist Information Brochure (1995) Druk Dimograf Bielska-Biala.

Paiss, J., quoted in Polakoff, J. (1993) 'Washington wrap up – US rejected money from Germany to help finance Holocaust Memorial Museum', *Intermountain Jewish News*, 9 April, p. 6.

Palmer, G. (1993) *Death: The Trip of a Lifetime*, New York: HarperCollins.

Pantcheff, T. (1991) *Alderney Fortress Island: The Germans in Alderney*, London: Fillimore.

Parker, S. (1976) *The Sociology of Leisure*, London: Allen & Unwin.

Pastal, B. and Abramson, S. H. (1971) *The Travellers Guide to Jewish Landmarks of Europe*, London: Fleet Press.

Piper, F. (1992) *Auschwitz – How many perished? – Jews, Poles, Gypsies*, Oswieczim: State Museum Auschwitz.

Polakoff, J. (1993) 'Washington wrap up – US rejected money from Germany to help finance Holocaust Memorial Museum', *Intermountain Jewish News*, 9 April, p. 6.

Posey, J. (1988) 'Dart and the second gunman', *Inside Dallas*, 22 July, p. 22.

Prentice, R. (1993) *Tourism and Heritage Attractions*, London: Routledge.

Price, C. (1994) Interview with Marketing Director, The Sixth Floor, Dallas, Texas, by the authors, 14 November.

Radford, D. (1995) 'Covering up the past', *Museums Journal*, Vol. 6, No. 1, pp. 29–31.

Rawecki, M. (1995) 'Protected zone', *Pro-Memoria*, Nos 1–2, January, pp. 29–33.

Read, M. (1991) 'Kennedy Museum's Sixth Floor', *Dallas Times Herald*, 20 April, p. A1.

Reid, A. (1995) *I M Pei*, Bison Group.

Richards, G. (ed.) (1995) *Cultural Tourism in Europe*, Wallingford: CAB.

Richards, P. (1993) 'Science = death. A requiem for the past, a warning for the future', *The Washington Post*, 18 April, pp. G1–G6.

Rogoff , I. (ed.) (1994) *Museum Culture: Histories, Discourse, Spectacles*, London: Routledge, pp 223–49.

Rojek, C. (1993a) *Ways of Escape*, Basingstoke: Macmillan.

Rojek, C. (1993b) *Ways of Seeing: Modern Transformations in Leisure and Travel*, Basingstoke: Macmillan.

Romney, J. (1995) 'Screen seen: vital video – The Holocaust', *The Guardian Weekly*, 13 January, p. T016.

Rosen, T. C. (1993) 'The misguided Holocaust Museum', *The New York Times*, op-ed, 18 April, p. 01.

Rosenfeld, A. (1980) *A Double Dying: Reflections on Holocaust Literature*, Bloomington: Indiana University Press.

Roskies, D. (1988) *The Literature of Destruction: Jewish Responses to Catastrophe*, Philadelphia: Bell University Press.

Roth, J. K. and Berenbaum, M. (eds) (1989) *Holocaust – Religious and Philosophical Implications*, London: Paragon House.

Rürup, R. (1989) *The Topography of Terror: A Documentation*, Berlin: Verlag Willmuth Arenhövel.

Rürup, R. (ed.) (1995) *Berlin, 1945* Berlin: Verlag Willmuth Arenhövel.

Sachsenhausen Memorial Centre (1995) *Guide and Information*, Sachsenhausen.

Schadeberg, J. (1994) *Voices from Robben Island*, Randberg: Raven Press.

Schwartz, K. D. (1993) 'Mutimedia walks museum visitors through Holocaust events', *Government Computer News*, 26 April, p. 5.

Seaton, A. V. (1996) 'Guided by the dark: from thanatopsis to thanatourism', *International Journal of Heritage Studies*, Vol. 2, No. 4, pp. 234–44.

Segev, T. (1993) *The Seventh Million – Jews in Israel during WWII*, New York: Hill & Wang.

Sherman, D. and Rogoff, I. (1994) *From Ruins to Debris: The Faminization of Fascism in German History Museums*, London: Routledge.

Slackman, M. (no date) *Remembering Pearl Harbor: The Story of the USS Arizona Memorial* (expanded edition), *Arizona* Memorial Museum Association.

Smolen, K. (1993) *State Museum in Oswieczim*, Krakow.

Star-Bulletin (1990) '*Arizona* Memorial tour accused of bias', Thursday, 18 October, 1990.

Steiner, G. (1967) *Language and Silence: Essays in Language, Literature and the Inhuman*, New York: Athenaeum.

Steiner, G. (1971) *In Bluebeard's Castle: Some Notes Towards the Redefinition of Culture*, New Haven, CT: Yale University Press.

Stevens, T. (1995) 'Heritage and design: a practitioner's perspective', in Herbert, D. (ed.) *Heritage, Tourism and Society*, London: Mansell.

Straits Times (1996) 'One section in Nagasaki museum may raise questions', Saturday, 23 March, 1996.

Sudnow, D. (1967) *Passing on the Social Organization of Dying*, Englewood Cliffs, NJ: Prentice-Hall.

Swiebocka, T. (1995) 'Auschwitz, yesterday and today', *Pro-Memoria*, Nos 1–2, January, pp. 3–5.

Tabb, P. (1995) Interview with Public Relations Consultant/Public Affairs Manager Sanctuary Inns and Daisy Hill Real Estate (Operators of the German Underground Hospital Museum) by the authors.

Thompson, B. D. (1992) *US Military Museums, Historic Sites and Exhibits*, Washington, DC: Military Living Publications.

Toms, C. (1967) *Hitler's Fortress Islands*, London: Collins.

Tourist Information (1997) *North Cyprus*, Gazimagusa: Tourist Information Publication.

TRNC (1996), *Tourism Statistical Yearbook 1996*, TRNC Government.

Tuchel, J. (1992) *House of the Wannsee Conference Permanent Exhibit* (English version), Berlin.

Tuchel, J. and Hoch, H. (1990) *German Resistance Memorial Centre*, Berlin: Museumtechnik.

Urry, J. (1990) *The Tourist Gaze*, London: Sage.

Urry, J. (1995) *Consuming Places*, London: Routledge.

US Army Chemical Corps Museum (no date) *Welcome to the US Army Chemical Corps Museum*, The Museum.

Uzzel, D. (1989) *Heritage Interpretation*, London: Belhaven.

Vellas, F. and Becherel, L. (1995) *International Tourism*, Basingstoke: Macmillan.

Waites, B. (ed.) (1993) *Europe and the Wider World*, London: Routledge.

Walsh, S. (1992) *The Representation of the Past*, London: Routledge.

Walter, T. (1996) 'Ritualising death in a consumer society', *Royal Society of Arts Journal*, Vol. CXLIV, No. 5468, April, pp. 32–40.

Webber, J. (1992) 'The future of Auschwitz', First Frank Green Lecture, Oxford Centre for Post-Graduate Hebrew Studies.

Welcome to Cyprus (1997) Nicosia: Republic of Cyprus.

Weinberg, E. (1993) 'Editorial – Holocaust Museum never again', *The Economist*, 1 May, p. 118.

White, T. (1960) *The Making of the President*, London and New York: Athenaeum.

White, T. (1982) *America in Search of Itself*, New York: Warner.

Wiesel, E. (1960) *Night*, transl. by S. Rodway, New York: Avon.

Wiesel, E. (1968) *Legends of our Fire*, transl. by S. Donadio, New York: Holt, Reinhart & Winston.

Wieseltier, L. (1993) 'After memory: reflection on the Holocaust Memorial Museum', *The New Republic*, 3 May, pp. 16–26.

Wilson, K. and Van der Dussen, L. (1993) *The History and Idea of Europe*, London: Routledge.

Witt, S. (1991) 'Tourism in Cyprus', *Tourism Management*, March, pp. 37–46.

WTO (1997) *Tourism Highlights 1997*, Madrid: WTO.

WTTC (1995) *World Travel and Tourism Council: Travel and Tourism Research Edition*, Oxford: Pergamon.

Wurmstedt, R. (1987) 'Towering issue', *Dallas Morning News*, 31 August, p. 1.1.

Wyschogrod, M. (1975) 'Some theological reflections on the Holocaust', *Response*, Vol. 25 (Spring), pp. 237–48.

Yayinlari, Turizin A. and North Cyprus Museum Friends (1995) *North Cyprus: Mosaic of Cultures*, North Cyprus: A. Turizin Yayinlari Ltd.

Yerushalmi, Y. H. (1982) *Zakhor: Jewish history and Jewish Memory*, Washington, DC: University of Washington Press.

Young, J. E. (1988) *Writing and Rewriting the Holocaust*, Bloomington: Indiana University Press.

Young, J. E. (1993) *The Texture of Memory: Holocaust Memorials and Meaning*, New Haven, CT: Yale University Press.

Young, J. E. (ed.) (1994) *The Art of Memory: Holocaust Memorials in History*, New York: Prestel.

Zelizer, B. (1992) *Covering the Body: The Kennedy Assassination, the Media and the Shaping of Collective Memory*, Chicago: University of Chicago Press.

Zeller, F. (1988) *When Time Ran Out*, New York: Permanent Press.

Index

Active Museum of Fascism
  and Resistance,
  Berlin   34–5
Alderney *see* Channel
  Islands
*All Quiet on the Western
  Front*   9
Altamont Racetrack   10,
  148
American Civil War   8
American Indians   158
'ancient', the   148
Anne Frank House   28
anxiety   11, 12, 16, 17,
  21–3, 24
Apocalypse Now   9
Arlington National
  Cemetery   78, 79, 80,
  88, 90
Armenians, persecution of
  21
Arromanches   125
artefacts   18, 22, 59, 81,
  83, 115, 116, 120
assassination   6, 9–11, 16,
  17, 67, 77–98, 112
Atlantic Wall   102, 125
'atomic tourism'   166
'attractions'   3, 26, 148
Auschwitz   24–5, 28–30,
  46–53, 55–65, 112,
  120, 152, 166
Auschwitz Council   55
authenticity   50, 62–3, 81

Barbarian Museum *see*
  Museum of Barbarism,
  North Cyprus
Batterie de Longues   125
Battle of Britain   102

Battle of Hastings   5
Battle of Normandy   122,
  124–5
battle sites   4, 5, 9, 10, 12,
  25–6, 99, 122, 166
Battle of the Somme   8,
  123
Bayeux Tapestry   126
behaviour code   60
Belfast   119, 160–1
Belfast City Hall   160, 161
Belgium   5, 99, 100, 101,
  122–8
Belzec   30
Berlin   33–7, 40–5,
  111–13, 119, 122, 126
Berlin Wall   10, 33, 120,
  121
Birkenau   24, 29, 46–7,
  49–52, 55, 57–8, 62,
  64, 152, 166; *see also*
  Auschwitz
Black Museum, St
  Augustine   122–8
Bletchley Park   118
Bletchley Park Trust   118
'Blitz Experience', the   115
bombing   99, 102, 155
Borkum   69, 70
Braveheart   12
bridge over the River
  Kwai   10, 20
British Expeditionary
  Force   100, 122
Brzeszce   50
Brzezinka   46, 49
Bucharest   148, 164
Bukittingi   1, 2, 3, 6
bunkers   19, 33, 99, 148,
  167–8

Cabinet War Rooms   115
Cambodia   9
Canada   26, 101
Canterbury Cathedral   4
Canterbury Tales   4
Carter, President Jimmy
  148
Ceauşescu, Nicolae   164
celebration   89–91
cemeteries   4, 14, 26, 77,
  78, 90, 99, 123, 125
Challenger space shuttle
  88
Changi Gaol   10, 13, 108
Channel Islands   66–76,
  162
  Alderney   69, 70, 71
  Guernsey   67, 68, 69, 70
  Jersey   66, 68, 69, 71–2
Chappaquidick   17
Chaucer, Geoffrey   4
Checkpoint Charlie   19,
  113, 114, 120
Checkpoint Charlie
  Museum   19
Chelmno   30
Churchill, Winston   116,
  119
cinema   6, 22
cities   111, 120
Civil Rights Movement
  Monument,
  Montgomery,
  Alabama   158
codebreaking   118
Cold War   11, 19, 102,
  113, 120
Colditz   20
collaboration   67, 68,
  73–6

'collateral damage' 6, 22
commemoration 52, 53,
    55, 57, 109, 110, 124,
    125
commercialization 5, 12,
    86–7, 95, 120, 124
commodification 5, 6, 11,
    12, 33, 61, 90, 115,
    120, 141, 165, 167,
    168
Commonwealth War Graves
    Commission
    (CWGC) 5, 14, 26,
    122, 123, 124
communication
    technology 8, 11,
    16–21, 168
communications satellites
    8
concentration camps 9,
    10, 27–31, 33, 36, 149
    in Germany 39–45
    in Poland 46–65
    liberation of 110
Cook, Thomas 7
cooperation 67, 68, 73
Crimean War 8
crimes against humanity
    75
Croatia 160, 164
Cromwell Street,
    Gloucester 66, 160,
    168
Cronkite, Walter 16, 78
Cu Chi tunnels 163
Czech Republic 31, 71

Dachau 28, 39–40; 64,
    149
Dallas Country Historical
    Foundation 82, 84,
    85, 86, 91, 93, 97
Dallas Country Historical
    Museum 96
Dallas Onward 94
D-Day campaign 124,
    164
Dealey Plaza 83, 92, 94,
    95, 98
Dean, James 10, 168
Death Park, Philippines
    77
Death Wall 57
decay 59, 61–3, 140
de-differentiation 90
demilitarized zone (DMZ),
    Cyprus 137, 140,
    141

Denktash, Rauf 141
development 32, 34, 45,
    71–2, 91–8, 140, 143,
    167
Diana, Princess of Wales
    6, 10, 17, 164, 168
direct mail 149
distortions 31, 50
documentation 28, 29,
    57, 111, 120
Dover Castle 118–19
doubt 11, 12, 16, 17,
    21–3, 24
Dresden 22, 110
Dubrovnik 119
Dunblane 10
Dunkirk 102, 118
Duxford Airfield 116, 117
Dynamic Earth Centre,
    Edinburgh 165

East Germany 19, 20, 31,
    40–2, 119; see also
    Germany
education 7, 9, 38–9, 84,
    119, 153, 156–7, 163
Eisenhower, Dwight 22,
    155
England 110–22
English Heritage 118
Enigma 118
'Enola Gay' exhibition
    18–19, 109
enosis 137, 138
EPCOT Center 165
eternal flame, Arlington
    78, 80, 88, 89
ethnic cleansing 119

'fatal attractions' 3
Ferdinand, Archduke of
    Austria 100
films 8, 9, 17, 18, 27, 30,
    79
final solution see Holocaust,
    Jewish
First World War 8, 10,
    164, 166
    commodification of 115
    exhibits in Imperial War
    Museum 11, 114–15
    significance for dark
    tourism 100–3
    sites in France and
    Belgium 25–6, 122–8
    war graves 11
    war sites 99–128

'forbidden zone' see
    demilitarized zone
    (DMZ), Cyprus
forced labour 67, 69
Ford Theater, Washington
    87
fortifications 66, 67, 74,
    147
Fortress Guernsey
    campaign 67
France 5, 26, 99, 100,
    101, 102, 122–8
fraternization 67, 76
Friends of Northern
    Cyprus 130

Gallipoli 9
Gandhi, Mahatma 19,
    113
'gaze' 3
Gedenkstätte Plötensee
    memorial 112
genocide 31, 38
genocide monuments 28
geographical factors in dark
    tourism 119
German Underground
    Hospital Museum 67,
    68, 69, 71, 76
Germany 10, 26, 33–45,
    101, 102, 110–22, 146,
    149–1; see also East
    Germany
Gestapo Gelände 33–5,
    45
Gestapo Museum, Berlin
    3
Gorbachev, Mikhail 103
Graceland 5
'grand tour' 7
graves 4, 14, 123, 125
Greece 130, 138, 139
Greek Cypriots 129, 130,
    132, 137, 138, 139,
    141, 144
Gross-Rosen 46
Guernsey see Channel
    Islands
Gulf War 6

Hall of Remembrance 151
Helgoland 69
Hellfire Corner 118
Himmler, Heinrich 34
Hiroshima 10, 18, 22,
    102, 104, 110, 111,
    164

Hiroshima Peace
  Memorial   110
Hitler, Adolf   26, 87, 102,
  112, 146, 148
Holocaust, Jewish   9, 11,
  21, 23–5, 27–65, 108,
  111–12, 119, 145–61,
  163, 166, 169; see also
  US Holocaust
  Memorial Museum
Holocaust Memorial
  Council   149
Holt, Tonie   25, 26
Holt's Battlefield Tours
  25, 122, 124
Hotensleben   120, 122
hydrogen bombs   102, 104

iconocentrism   148
ID admission card   146,
  152, 156
ideology   19, 31, 41–2, 52,
  106–7, 112, 119, 120,
  136
IG Farben works   46, 50
Imperial War Museum   11,
  19, 67, 68–9, 113, 117,
  121, 159
imprisonment sites   147
International Auschwitz
  Committee (IAC)   60,
  62
Internet   169
interpretation   151–9, 162,
  166
  Channel Island
    occupation   66–76
  Cyprus demilitarized
    zone   137
  Cyprus dispute   141,
    144
  Gestapo Gelände   33,
    35
  Jewish Holocaust sites
    23, 24, 25, 27, 28, 31,
    39, 46, 51–3, 55–63
  Normandy   128
  Sachsenhausen   112
  Second World War   109,
    115–16
  at visitor centres   148
  Wannsee Conference
    house   38, 39
Ireland see Northern Ireland
Island Fortress Occupation
  Museum, St Helier
  73
Israel   158

Japan   103–10, 126, 163
Japanese   1, 2, 6, 13, 14,
  103–10
Jersey see Channel Islands
Jersey Experience   73
Jersey Museum   73
Jersey Tourism   66–7, 73
JFK   9, 91
JFK Presidential Limousine
  Tour   98
John F. Kennedy Library,
  Boston   78, 80, 81,
  85, 86, 89, 91
Johnny Got His Gun   9

Keneally, Thomas   64
Kennedy cenotaph   159
Kennedy Edward   85
Kennedy Jacqueline   78,
  85
Kennedy, John F.   6, 10,
  11, 16, 17, 67, 77–98,
  164, 168
Kennedy Memorial   92
Kennedy, Robert   17, 80,
  88
King, Martin Luther   10,
  11, 87, 113
Konavia   160
Korean War Memorial,
  Washington, DC   14,
  15, 16
Koreans   109
Krakow   30, 63, 64
Kulaks   158
Kyrenia   140

Lamsdorf   46
landscape   100, 124, 125,
  146, 167
Langemarck   123
Lanzmann, Claude   25,
  30–1, 156
Lauder, Donald   58
League of Nations   101
Lepong Japang   1–3
liberal democracy   11, 109
liberation   40, 69, 73, 74,
  110, 125, 155
Liberation Memorial
  Sculpture, St Helier
  72, 73
Lidice   54
Lincoln, Abraham   87
Little Rock, Arkansas   22
Live Aid   6
'Living History Tour',
  Belfast   160–1

location   91
logocentrism   148
London   119, 120, 122,
  126
Lorraine Motel, Memphis
  87
Lynn, Dame Vera   118

Majdanek   28, 30, 32, 46
Martin-Gropius-Bau   111
Marxism-Leninism   19,
  23, 55, 112
mass tourism   9, 10
mausoleums   4
media   5–6, 8, 16–21, 30,
  32, 147, 151–9, 164,
  167
megali   138
memorabilia   74
memorialization   3, 4
memorials   49, 57, 99,
  104–8, 123, 146–7
memory   12, 66, 67, 82,
  99, 146, 155
Menin Gate Memorial
  122, 124
Mesaoria Plain   140
meta-narratives   11, 21–3,
  24
misrepresentation   52
modernity   7, 8, 11, 12,
  21, 22, 148
Monowitz   46, 49
Monroe, Marilyn   10
monuments   124, 147,
  158–9
Morrison, Jim   77
multi-culturalism   5
multimedia   152
murals   161
Murphy, Audie   88
Musée de la Libération,
  Cherbourg   125
Musée des Épaves Sous-
  marines du
  Débarquement   125
Musée du Mur de
  l'Atlantique,
  Ouistreham   125
Musée Mémorial de la
  Bataille de Normandie,
  Bayeux   125
Musée pour la Paix, Caen
  125, 126
Museum of Barbarism
  (Barbarian Museum),
  North Cyprus   141,
  143

Museum of Human
    Genocide, Cambodia
    25, 163
Museum of the Atrocity,
    North Cyprus 137
Museum of the National
    Dispute, North
    Cyprus 136
Museum of Tolerance, Los
    Angeles 21, 64, 150,
    151

Nagasaki 22, 102, 104,
    110, 164
Nagasaki Atomic Bomb
    Museum 109
Nashville Museum of John
    F. Kennedy
    Memorabilia 92
National Dispute Museum,
    North Cyprus 141
National History
    Curriculum 116, 119
National Maritime
    Museum, Greenwich
    18
National Parks Service
    105, 106
nationalization of sites 37
NATO 103
New Museum, JFK Library,
    Boston 78, 80
newsreels 17, 89, 90, 152
Nicosia (Lefkosa) 137,
    141
Night to Remember, A 8,
    18
Norderney 69, 71
Normandy 102, 122–8,
    164
North Atlantic Treaty
    Organization
    (NATO) 103
North Cyprus 129–44
    border with south see
    demilitarized zone
    (DMZ)
    employees in tourism in
    135
    mail to 136
    maps of 138, 141
    market development in
    133–4, 136–40
    military impact on 140
    room occupancy rates
    in 134, 139
    tourist arrivals in
    130–3, 141

tourist guides 136, 138
tourist income in 134,
    139
transport difficulties
    131–2
Turkish invasion 137–8
Turkish visitors to 141,
    143
North Korea 137
Northern Ireland 11, 160,
    163

Oklahoma City bombing
    10
Olympia Stadium, Berlin
    45
Omaha Beach 16, 126
Open Air Museum of the
    Battle of Normandy
    124
Organisation Todt (OT)
    67, 69–71, 73
Oswald, Lee Harvey 16,
    78, 79, 84, 87, 91–2,
    94
Oswieczim see Auschwitz

Pacific war 103–10, 113
Palestinians 158
Pearl Harbor 10, 102,
    104–8, 125
Phoenix, River 10
photographs 8, 28–9, 44,
    61, 111, 112, 151
pilgrimage 3, 4, 148
planning 11, 21, 22
Plötzensee Prison 36–7
Pol Pot 125
Poland 10, 31, 46–65,
    157
post-modernity 11, 90,
    103, 145, 146, 147,
    148
Powiak Prison 46
Precious Gold Mountain,
    Taiwan 77
presentation 5, 6, 31, 167
preservation 59, 61–2
Presley, Elvis 5, 10
Princip, Gavrilo 100
'privacy walls' 151, 156
Punch Bowl, Honolulu 16

Radogoszcz 46
Rajsko 50
Ravensbrück 45
'reality gap' 156

'real time' 30, 31
reconstruction 30, 35, 84,
    116, 122
remembrance 3, 4, 14, 18,
    26, 103, 146, 147, 151,
    155, 164, 166
replication 30, 115, 152
representation 31, 120,
    146, 167
Republic of Cyprus
    (southern Cyprus)
    130, 138, 139, 141,
    143
'respect' 10, 77, 105
'resurrection' 29
reverence 26, 57, 77, 88,
    89–91, 112, 156, 166,
    167
revisionism 103, 106,
    109, 153, 154
rhetorical legitimation 80
River Kwai 10, 20, 108
'Rodney King' affair 21
Roosevelt, Franklin
    Delano 106
Roswell, New Mexico
    167
Roswell Incident, The 167
Russian Revolution 101

Sachsenhausen 23, 40–5,
    112, 120
'sacred cow' concept 119
Saigon 111
Sarajevo 159, 160, 164
Saudi Arabia 148
Saving Private Ryan 126,
    169
Schindler's Ark 64
Schindler's List 6, 25, 30,
    64
'Schindler Tour' 30, 64
Schlieffen Plan 100
school trips 122
science, failures of 11
'screen time' 31
sculpture 152
Second World War
    Channel Islands during
    66–76
    documentation of 29
    exhibits in Imperial War
    Museum 11
    Lepong Japang tunnels
    1–3
    Japanese occupation of
    Singapore 13, 108

Pacific war 103–10
significance for dark tourism 100–3
social life in 119
Soviet role in 153
war sites 99–128
see also Holocaust, Jewish
Securitate 148
Selma, Alabama 10
service industries 5
Shoah 9, 25, 30
Simon Wiesenthal Center 21
Singapore 10, 13, 108, 111
Sixth Floor, the 66, 78, 80, 82–7, 89, 90, 91–7, 98, 159, 164
Smithsonian Air and Space Exhibition 18
Smithsonian Institute 108
Sobibor 30
Somme 26, 126, 166
South Africa 19
South Korea 137
southern Cyprus see Republic of Cyprus
Southern Poverty Law Center 158
souvenirs 2
Soviet internment 42, 44
Spanish Civil War 111
Speer, Albert 45
Spielberg, Steven 25, 30, 64
St Louis 155
St Peter's Bunker 73
St Peter's village 73
Stutthof 46
Switzerland 101
Sylt 69, 71

Tate, Sharon 10
technology 8, 18, 20, 22, 109, 113, 152, 163; see also communication technology

television 6, 8, 16, 17, 20, 27, 78, 79, 81–2, 89, 147
Terezin 71
Texas Book Depository Building 82, 86, 92, 96, 140
Texas Historical Commission 86
texts 27
Thailand 108
theatres 151
Third Reich 27–45
Thomas à Becket 4
Tiananmen Square 20, 113, 163
'time relation', the 29, 30
Titanic cruises 18, 165
Titanic (film) 6, 18, 165, 169
Titanic (ship) 8, 11, 17, 18, 165, 166
'Topography of Terrors' 34, 70, 111
Tora, Tora, Tora 104
torture cells 34, 119
Treblinka 30, 46
Trench, The 9
Trench Experience, the 113–15, 159
trench warfare 101
Trzebinia 50
Tudjman, Franjo 154
Turkey 129, 130, 131. 136, 137, 141, 143
Turkish Cypriots 129, 137, 144
Turkish Republic of North Cyprus (TRNC) see North Cyprus

Ulster Museum 160
undertakers 5
United States 101
universal suffrage 7
universalism 7
US Army Chemical Corps Museum, Fort McClellan 109

US Holocaust Memorial Museum 10, 25, 31, 64, 122, 145–61
USS Arizona Memorial 104–8

Varosha 140
VE Day 110
Vichy government 102
video 18, 85
Vietnam War 10, 16, 163
Vietnam War Memorial, Washington, DC 14, 15, 16, 159
Vimy Ridge 123
VJ Day 110

Wannsee Conference House 37–9, 111–12
Warren Commission 17
Wars of Independence, Scottish 12
Warsaw citadel 46
Warsaw ghetto 32, 152
'Washington experience' the 151
Watergate 20, 148, 168
West, the 10, 163
West, Fred and Rosemary 66, 168
West Sumatra 1
Wexner Learning Centre 151
Winston Churchill's Britain at War Experience 116, 118, 120
Wulf, Joseph 37

Yamamoto, Admiral Isoroku 105
Ypres 122, 124
Yugoslavia 158, 159

Zagan 46
Zamosk Rotunda 46
Zeppelins 101
Zyklon B exhibit 57